AI N.L.P.
PROMPT MASTER

CLASS TEXTBOOK

BY: DR. JOSEPH G. MUCHA, J.D.
A.I. PROMPT DOCTOR

MASTER DEGREE
CLASS TEXTBOOK

TABLE OF CONTENTS

CHAPTER 1
INTRODUCTION TO CHATGPT
PROMPT MASTER

Welcome to the ChatGPT Prompt Master Class! In this class, you will learn how to use ChatGPT Prompt Master, a powerful tool that can generate high-quality text based on your input prompts.

As a master-level student at ChatGPT School, you have already demonstrated your proficiency in language generation, but ChatGPT Prompt Master will take your skills to the next level.

With ChatGPT Prompt Master, you will be able to generate text for a wide variety of applications, from creative writing to marketing copy to summarizing long documents.

This tool is designed to help you optimize your language generation skills and improve your efficiency and effectiveness as a text generator.

In this textbook, you will learn everything you need to know about ChatGPT Prompt Master, including its capabilities, how to use it, and advanced techniques for getting the most out of this tool.

You will receive a step-by-step guide to using ChatGPT Prompt Master, along with tips and tricks for optimizing your prompts and fine-tuning the model.

Whether you are a professional writer, a marketer, or simply someone who enjoys generating high-quality text, ChatGPT Prompt Master will be an invaluable tool in your toolkit.

By mastering the use of this tool, you will become a more proficient text generator and take your language generation skills to the next level. So, let's get started and explore the world of ChatGPT Prompt Master together.

Review of ChatGPT Prompt Practitioner and ChatGPT Prompt Engineer Concepts

Before we dive into the Master Class, it's important to review the concepts of ChatGPT Prompt Practitioner and ChatGPT Prompt Engineer, which are the prerequisite courses to this class.

These courses have laid the foundation for your language generation skills and have prepared you to work with more advanced language generation tools like ChatGPT Prompt Master.

In the ChatGPT Prompt Practitioner course, you learned the basics of language generation using the GPT model.

You learned how to input prompts, adjust the settings, and interpret the output. You also learned some best practices for generating high-quality text and avoiding common mistakes.

In the ChatGPT Prompt Engineer course, you took your language generation skills to the next level. You learned how to fine-tune the GPT model to produce text that is tailored to your specific needs.

You learned how to optimize your prompts for best results, how to use different settings to achieve different goals, and how to evaluate the output to ensure its quality.

Now, in the ChatGPT Prompt Master Class, you will apply these concepts and take them to the next level with the more advanced ChatGPT Prompt Master tool.

You will learn how to use this tool to generate text for a wide variety of applications, including creative writing, marketing copy, and summarizing long documents. You will learn how to use advanced techniques to optimize your prompts and fine-tune the model for best results.

By mastering these concepts, you will become a proficient text generator and be able to generate high-quality text with ease. So let's review the concepts of ChatGPT Prompt Practitioner and ChatGPT Prompt Engineer and get ready to take your language generation skills to the next level with ChatGPT Prompt Master.

The ChatGPT Prompt Practitioner course introduced you to the basics of language generation using the GPT model. You learned how to input prompts and adjust the settings to generate text that is relevant to your requirements. You also learned how to evaluate the output and identify the common mistakes to avoid.

In the course, you learned that the success of generating text with the GPT model depends on several factors, including the quality of the prompt, the size of the model, and the relevance of the training data. You also learned that different settings could affect the output, such as the length of the output, the temperature, and the repetition penalty.

The ChatGPT Prompt Engineer course took your skills to the next level by teaching you how to fine-tune the GPT model to generate text that is more specific to your needs.

You learned how to optimize your prompts by adding context and constraints, and how to use different settings to achieve different goals. You also learned how to evaluate the output and identify areas of improvement.

You learned that the key to fine-tuning the GPT model is to have a well-defined objective and a specific set of requirements. You also learned how to adjust the hyperparameters of the model, such as the learning rate and the number of epochs, to optimize its performance.

Now, in the ChatGPT Prompt Master Class, you will build on the concepts learned in the previous courses and take them to the next level. You will learn how to use ChatGPT Prompt Master, a more advanced tool, to generate text that is relevant to your needs.

In this class, you will learn how to use ChatGPT Prompt Master to generate text for a wide variety of applications, such as creative writing, marketing copy, and summarizing long documents.

You will learn how to use advanced techniques to optimize your prompts, such as adding context and constraints, and how to fine-tune the model to achieve the desired output.

You will also learn how to use ChatGPT Prompt Master to generate text in different languages, such as Chinese and French, and how to use it to generate text in specific domains, such as law and medicine. You will also learn how to use the tool in combination with other language generation tools to achieve even better results.

By mastering the concepts of ChatGPT Prompt Practitioner and ChatGPT Prompt Engineer, and by learning how to use ChatGPT Prompt Master, you will become a proficient text generator and be able to generate high-quality text with ease.

So let's get started and take your language generation skills to the next level and become a ChatGPT Prompt Master.

Overview of the Role of a
ChatGPT Prompt Master

As a ChatGPT Prompt Master, your role is to use the language generation skills you've acquired through the previous courses to generate high-quality text that meets specific requirements. You will be responsible for creating content that is relevant, informative, and engaging, whether it's for marketing copy, creative writing, or summarizing long documents.

Your primary responsibility is to optimize the use of ChatGPT Prompt Master to generate text that meets your client's needs. This may require you to fine-tune the model, adjust the settings, and optimize the prompts to achieve the desired output. You will need to have a strong understanding of the different hyperparameters, such as the learning rate, the number of epochs, and the size of the model, to be able to fine-tune the model effectively.

You will also need to be familiar with various techniques to optimize your prompts, such as adding context, constraints, and other relevant information. This will ensure that the generated text is both relevant and informative. You will need to be able to evaluate the output of the model and identify areas for improvement.

In addition to generating text, you may also be responsible for providing guidance and support to other team members or clients. You may be required to explain the process of generating text using ChatGPT Prompt Master and help others fine-tune the model or optimize their prompts.

To be successful as a ChatGPT Prompt Master, you will need to have a deep understanding of the GPT model and how it works, as well as strong language generation skills. You will also need to be able to communicate effectively with clients and team members and be able to work well under pressure to meet tight deadlines.

The role of a ChatGPT Prompt Master is critical in generating high-quality text that meets specific requirements. As a master of language generation, you will play a key role in helping clients and organizations achieve their goals through the power of words.

Here are some additional details on the role of a ChatGPT Prompt Master:

Understanding Client Needs:
As a ChatGPT Prompt Master, you will need to have a deep understanding of your client's needs and goals. This may involve working closely with clients to identify their specific requirements, such as tone, style, and length of the text. You will need to be able to ask the right questions to get a clear understanding of what the client wants and needs.

Generating High-Quality Text:
Your primary responsibility will be to generate high-quality text that meets the client's requirements. This may involve using ChatGPT Prompt Master to generate text from scratch, or it may involve optimizing existing text to make it more relevant and informative. You will need to be able to evaluate the output of the model and make adjustments as needed to achieve the desired results.

Fine-Tuning The Model:
To generate high-quality text, you will need to have a strong understanding of how the GPT model works and be able to fine-tune it effectively. This may involve adjusting the hyperparameters, such as the learning rate and the number of epochs, to optimize the performance of the model. You may also need to experiment with different settings to achieve the desired results.

Optimizing Prompts:
In addition to fine-tuning the model, you will also need to be able to optimize your prompts to achieve the desired output. This may involve adding context, constraints, and other relevant information to the prompt to ensure that the generated text is both relevant and informative. You will need to have a deep understanding of the different techniques for optimizing prompts and be able to apply them effectively.

Providing guidance and support:
As a ChatGPT Prompt Master, you may be required to provide guidance and support to other team members or clients. This may involve explaining the process of generating text using ChatGPT Prompt Master and helping others fine-tune the model or optimize their prompts. You will need to be able to communicate effectively with clients and team members and be able to work collaboratively to achieve the desired results.

Providing expert guidance:
A ChatGPT Prompt Master provides expert guidance and feedback to writers, helping them to improve their writing skills and develop their own unique writing style.

Developing effective prompts:
A ChatGPT Prompt Master creates engaging and thought-provoking prompts that challenge writers to think outside the box and explore new ideas and perspectives.

Encouraging creativity:
A ChatGPT Prompt Master encourages writers to tap into their creativity and imagination, helping them to find new and innovative ways to express themselves through their writing.

Fostering a supportive community:
A ChatGPT Prompt Master creates a supportive and inclusive environment where writers can share their work, receive feedback, and collaborate with one another.

Providing constructive criticism:
A ChatGPT Prompt Master provides constructive criticism and feedback to writers, helping them to identify areas for improvement and refine their writing skills.

Inspiring Writers:
A ChatGPT Prompt Master inspires writers to push themselves beyond their comfort zones and explore new ideas and themes in their writing.

Offering Writing Exercises:
A ChatGPT Prompt Master provides writing exercises and prompts that help writers to practice and refine their skills, allowing them to grow and develop as writers.

Curating Resources:
A ChatGPT Prompt Master curates a range of writing resources and tools that help writers to improve their craft, from grammar and style guides to writing workshops and online courses.

Supporting Professional Development:
A ChatGPT Prompt Master supports writers in their professional development, providing advice on how to build a writing career, find clients, and market their work.

Providing A Platform For Writers:
A ChatGPT Prompt Master provides a platform for writers to showcase their work, connect with other writers and readers, and gain exposure for their writing.

The role of a ChatGPT Prompt Master is critical in generating high-quality text that meets specific requirements.

To be successful in this role, you will need to have a deep understanding of the GPT model and how it works, as well as strong language generation skills.

You will also need to be able to work well under pressure to meet tight deadlines and be able to communicate effectively with clients and team members.

Understanding the Technical Requirements
for Building State-of-the-Art ChatGPT Models

Building state-of-the-art ChatGPT models requires a strong understanding of the technical requirements involved in the process.

These requirements include the hardware and software resources needed, the data collection and preparation process, the model architecture, and the training process.

Hardware And Software Requirements:

Building state-of-the-art ChatGPT models requires access to powerful hardware and software resources. The hardware requirements for training large models are typically high-end GPUs or TPUs.

The software requirements include deep learning frameworks such as TensorFlow or PyTorch, as well as access to cloud computing resources for training and inference.

Data Collection And Preparation:

To train state-of-the-art ChatGPT models, it is important to have access to large and diverse datasets that are representative of the domain of interest.

The data must be cleaned and preprocessed to remove any noise or inconsistencies, and the data must be labeled and annotated to enable supervised or unsupervised training.

Model Architecture:

The architecture of the ChatGPT model is critical to its performance. The model should be designed to handle the complexity and nuances of natural language processing tasks, including text generation, summarization, and classification.

The model should include attention mechanisms, recurrent neural networks, and other advanced techniques to improve its performance.

Training Process:
The training process for ChatGPT models involves fine-tuning pre-trained models on large and diverse datasets. The process involves tuning the model hyperparameters, such as the learning rate and batch size, to achieve optimal performance.

The training process is iterative and may take several days or weeks to complete, depending on the size of the model and the size of the training dataset.

In addition to these technical requirements, building state-of-the-art ChatGPT models requires a deep understanding of natural language processing concepts and techniques. It also requires expertise in deep learning, mathematics, and statistics.

Building state-of-the-art ChatGPT models is a challenging but rewarding process that can enable organizations to leverage the power of natural language processing to achieve their goals.

Here are some additional details on the technical requirements for building state-of-the-art ChatGPT models:

Hardware And Software Requirements:
The hardware requirements for training large ChatGPT models are typically high-end GPUs or TPUs with large amounts of memory.

These resources can be expensive, so many organizations use cloud computing services like Google Cloud, Amazon Web Services, or Microsoft Azure to train their models.

In addition to hardware, deep learning frameworks such as TensorFlow or PyTorch are essential for building and training ChatGPT models. These frameworks provide APIs for building models, running experiments, and performing model evaluations.

Data Collection And Preparation:

To train state-of-the-art ChatGPT models, it's important to have access to large and diverse datasets that are representative of the domain of interest.

These datasets can be sourced from a variety of sources, including web pages, social media platforms, news articles, and customer service logs.

Once data has been collected, it must be cleaned and preprocessed to remove any noise or inconsistencies. This can involve tasks like tokenization, stemming, and stop word removal.

The data must also be labeled and annotated to enable supervised or unsupervised training.

Model Architecture:

The architecture of a ChatGPT model plays a critical role in its performance. A typical architecture includes multiple layers of bidirectional transformer encoders and decoders, which are trained to predict the next word in a sequence given the previous words.

Attention mechanisms are used to weigh the importance of each word in the sequence, and dropout is used to prevent overfitting.

Training Process:

The training process for ChatGPT models involves fine-tuning pre-trained models on large and diverse datasets. Fine-tuning involves using the pre-trained model as a starting point and then training it on a smaller, more specialized dataset to adapt it to a specific domain.

The training process is iterative and may take several days or weeks to complete, depending on the size of the model and the size of the training dataset.

During training, it's important to monitor the model's performance using metrics like perplexity, accuracy, and F1 score. Hyperparameters like the learning rate, batch size, and optimizer must be tuned to achieve optimal performance.

Building state-of-the-art ChatGPT models requires access to powerful hardware and software resources, large and diverse datasets, a deep understanding of natural language processing concepts and techniques, and expertise in deep learning, mathematics, and statistics.

With the right tools and expertise, organizations can build powerful ChatGPT models that can be used for a wide range of applications, from customer service bots to content generation and more.

CHAPTER 2
ADVANCED NATURAL LANGUAGE PROCESSING TECHNIQUES

This chapter builds on the foundational concepts covered in Chapter 1 and focuses on advanced techniques in natural language processing (NLP).

These techniques can be used to improve the performance of ChatGPT models and enable more sophisticated applications.

Topic Modeling:
Topic modeling is a technique used to discover the underlying themes or topics in a corpus of text. This technique can be used to identify the key topics in a dataset of customer feedback, social media posts, or other types of text data.

ChatGPT models can be trained to generate responses that are specific to a particular topic or theme.

Sentiment Analysis:
Sentiment analysis is the process of identifying the emotional tone of a piece of text, such as positive, negative, or neutral. ChatGPT models can be trained to generate responses that are tailored to the emotional tone of the user's input.

For example, a ChatGPT model could generate a more empathetic response to a user who expresses frustration or sadness.

Named Entity Recognition:
Named entity recognition (NER) is the process of identifying and categorizing named entities in a piece of text, such as people, places, and organizations. ChatGPT models can be trained to generate responses that are specific to a named entity mentioned in the user's input.

For example, a ChatGPT model could generate a response about the weather in a particular city mentioned by the user.

Coreference Resolution:

Coreference resolution is the process of identifying when two or more words or phrases in a piece of text refer to the same entity. ChatGPT models can be trained to generate responses that take into account the user's previous statements and refer to entities mentioned earlier in the conversation.

Advanced Dialogue Management:

Advanced dialogue management techniques can be used to improve the flow and coherence of a conversation between a ChatGPT model and a user. Techniques like reinforcement learning and hierarchical modeling can be used to improve the ability of ChatGPT models to maintain a coherent and engaging conversation.

Word Embeddings:

This technique maps words to vectors in high-dimensional space, allowing algorithms to understand semantic relationships between words and phrases.

Machine Translation:

This technique automatically translates text from one language to another using statistical models or neural networks.

Text Summarization:

This technique automatically summarizes a large document into a shorter version, which can be useful in news articles, scientific papers, or legal documents.

Question Answering:

This technique automatically answers questions posed in natural language by retrieving information from a knowledge base or text corpus.

Speech Recognition:

This technique transcribes spoken language into text, allowing for the development of voice assistants, speech-to-text tools, and automated customer service systems.

Natural Language Generation:

This technique involves generating text from structured data, which can be useful in creating personalized emails, product descriptions, or news articles.

Coreference Resolution:

This technique identifies and resolves references to entities in a given text, such as pronouns and named entities, allowing for more accurate analysis of the text.

This chapter provides an overview of advanced NLP techniques that can be used to enhance the performance of ChatGPT models and enable more sophisticated applications.

By using these techniques, organizations can build ChatGPT models that are better equipped to handle the nuances and complexities of human language.

In-Depth Analysis of NLP Concepts such as Language Modeling, Semantic Representation, and Discourse Analysis

This chapter provides an in-depth analysis of key NLP concepts that are critical for building advanced ChatGPT models.

These concepts include language modeling, semantic representation, and discourse analysis.

Language Modeling:

Language modeling is the task of predicting the next word in a sequence of words. This is done by training a model on a large corpus of text data and using it to generate a probability distribution over the possible next words.

ChatGPT models use language modeling to generate responses to user input that are grammatically correct and semantically coherent.

Language modeling is the task of predicting the next word in a sequence of words. It is a fundamental problem in natural language processing and is used in a wide variety of applications, including machine translation, speech recognition, and text generation.

Language modeling is particularly important in the context of ChatGPT models, which generate responses to user input by predicting the next word in a conversation.

N-gram Language Modeling:
N-gram language modeling is a popular technique for building language models. An n-gram is a contiguous sequence of n items from a given sequence of text, where the items are typically words or characters.

For example, in the sentence "The cat sat on the mat," the bigram "cat sat" is a 2-gram and the trigram "the cat sat" is a 3-gram. N-gram language models estimate the probability of the next word in a sequence given the previous n-1 words.

Neural Language Modeling:
Neural language modeling is an alternative approach to building language models that has gained popularity in recent years. Neural language models use artificial neural networks to learn the probability distribution of the next word in a sequence given the previous words. The most common type of neural language model is the recurrent neural network (RNN), which is designed to process sequences of data. The long short-term memory (LSTM) network is a variant of the RNN that has been particularly successful in language modeling.

Evaluation of Language Models:
There are several metrics used to evaluate the performance of language models. The most common metric is perplexity, which measures how well a language model predicts a test set of data. A lower perplexity indicates that the language model is better at predicting the next word in a sequence. Other evaluation metrics include accuracy, precision, and recall.

Applications of Language Modeling:
Language modeling is used in a wide variety of natural language processing applications. In machine translation, language modeling is used to predict the next word in a translated sentence. In speech recognition, language modeling is used to predict the next word in a spoken sentence. In text generation, language modeling is used to generate coherent and semantically relevant text.

Language modeling is a fundamental problem in natural language processing and is used in a wide variety of applications. N-gram language modeling and neural language modeling are two popular approaches to building language models, and there are several metrics used to evaluate their performance.

By leveraging language modeling techniques, ChatGPT models can generate responses that are grammatically correct and semantically coherent.

Semantic Representation:

Semantic representation is the process of converting natural language text into a structured representation that can be easily processed by a computer. This involves identifying the meaning of words and phrases and mapping them to a set of concepts or entities. ChatGPT models use semantic representation to generate responses that are relevant to the user's input.

Semantic representation is the process of representing the meaning of words and phrases in a way that can be understood by machines. It is a fundamental problem in natural language processing and is used in a wide variety of applications, including sentiment analysis, question-answering, and chatbot development. Semantic representation is particularly important in the context of ChatGPT models, which generate responses to user input by understanding the meaning of the input.

Word Embeddings:
One of the most common techniques for semantic representation is word embeddings. Word embeddings are dense vector representations of words that capture their meaning in a high-dimensional space. Word embeddings are typically learned using unsupervised techniques, such as neural network-based models. Word embeddings have been shown to be effective in capturing semantic relationships between words, such as synonyms and antonyms.

Semantic Role Labeling:
Semantic role labeling is a technique for assigning semantic roles to words in a sentence. Semantic roles are the relationship between the words in a sentence and the actions or events that they describe.

For example, in the sentence "John ate a sandwich," the word "John" is the agent, the word "ate" is the predicate, and the word "sandwich" is the patient. Semantic role labeling is typically performed using supervised machine learning techniques.

Knowledge Graphs:
Knowledge graphs are a type of semantic representation that represent knowledge in a structured form. Knowledge graphs consist of nodes (representing entities) and edges (representing relationships between entities).

Knowledge graphs can be used to represent a wide variety of information, including facts, concepts, and relationships between entities. Knowledge graphs can be constructed using a combination of manual curation and automatic extraction techniques.

Evaluation of Semantic Representations:
There are several metrics used to evaluate the performance of semantic representations. The most common metric is accuracy, which measures how well the semantic representation captures the meaning of a word or phrase. Other evaluation metrics include precision and recall.

Applications of Semantic Representations:
Semantic representation is used in a wide variety of natural language processing applications. In sentiment analysis, semantic representations are used to understand the emotional content of text. In question-answering, semantic representations are used to match questions with relevant answers.

 In chatbot development, semantic representations are used to understand the meaning of user input and generate appropriate responses.

Semantic representation is a fundamental problem in natural language processing and is used in a wide variety of applications. Word embeddings, semantic role labeling, and knowledge graphs are three common techniques used for semantic representation.

By leveraging semantic representation techniques, ChatGPT models can generate responses that are not only grammatically correct but also semantically coherent and relevant to the user's input.

Discourse Analysis:

Discourse analysis is the study of how language is used to create meaning in a conversation. This involves analyzing the structure and context of a conversation to understand the intended meaning of the speaker.

ChatGPT models use discourse analysis to generate responses that are contextually appropriate and relevant to the ongoing conversation.

Discourse analysis is the study of how language is used in context, including the structure and organization of conversations, the use of language to convey meaning, and the social and cultural factors that influence communication.

Discourse analysis is important in natural language processing because it helps to understand the structure and meaning of conversations and can be used to improve the accuracy of language models.

Types of Discourse Analysis:
There are several types of discourse analysis, including conversation analysis, critical discourse analysis, and multimodal discourse analysis. Conversation analysis is focused on the structure and organization of conversations, while critical discourse analysis is focused on the social and cultural factors that influence communication.

Multimodal discourse analysis examines the use of multiple modes of communication, such as text, images, and sound.

Discourse Markers:

Discourse markers are words or phrases that signal the structure and organization of conversations. They are often used to mark transitions between different parts of a conversation, such as the introduction of a new topic or the conclusion of a discussion. Examples of discourse markers include "well," "so," and "anyway."

Discourse markers are important for natural language processing because they provide clues about the structure and meaning of conversations.

Speech Acts:

Speech acts are the actions performed by speakers through the use of language. Speech acts include statements, questions, and commands, among others.

Speech acts are important for natural language processing because they help to understand the intent behind the use of language. For example, a statement can be used to convey information, while a question can be used to elicit information.

Pragmatics:

Pragmatics is the study of how context influences the meaning of language. Pragmatics is important for natural language processing because it helps to understand the meaning of language beyond its literal interpretation. For example, the meaning of the sentence "Can you pass the salt?" depends on the context in which it is used.

In some contexts, it may be a polite request, while in other contexts it may be a sarcastic remark.

Applications of Discourse Analysis:
Discourse analysis is used in a wide variety of natural language processing applications. In sentiment analysis, discourse analysis can be used to understand the emotional content of conversations. In chatbot development, discourse analysis can be used to understand the structure and organization of conversations and generate appropriate responses.

Discourse analysis is an important field in natural language processing that helps to understand the structure and meaning of conversations. Discourse markers, speech acts, and pragmatics are three important concepts in discourse analysis.

By leveraging discourse analysis techniques, ChatGPT models can generate responses that are not only grammatically correct but also appropriate to the context and intent of the conversation.

Syntax and Semantics:

Syntax and semantics are two fundamental components of natural language. Syntax refers to the structure of language, including grammar, punctuation, and sentence construction. Semantics refers to the meaning of language, including word choice, context, and connotation.

ChatGPT models use both syntax and semantics to generate responses that are grammatically correct and semantically coherent.

Syntax and semantics are two fundamental concepts in natural language processing. Syntax is concerned with the structure and organization of sentences, while semantics is concerned with the meaning of sentences.

Together, syntax and semantics provide a framework for understanding the structure and meaning of language.

Syntax:
Syntax is the study of the rules that govern the structure and organization of sentences. Syntax is concerned with the arrangement of words and phrases to form grammatically correct sentences.

It includes the study of parts of speech, such as nouns, verbs, adjectives, and adverbs, as well as the study of sentence structure, such as subject-verb-object order.

The rules of syntax are important for natural language processing because they provide a framework for understanding the structure of language and generating grammatically correct sentences.

Semantics:

Semantics is the study of the meaning of language. Semantics is concerned with the relationships between words and phrases and the meanings they convey. It includes the study of word meanings, sentence meanings, and the relationships between sentences. The study of semantics is important for natural language processing because it provides a framework for understanding the meaning of language and generating appropriate responses.

Syntax-Semantics Interface:

The interface between syntax and semantics is an important area of study in natural language processing. The interface between syntax and semantics concerns how the structure of language relates to its meaning.

For example, the sentence "The cat chased the mouse" has a different meaning than "The mouse chased the cat" even though the words are arranged in the same order.

The study of the syntax-semantics interface is important for natural language processing because it provides a framework for understanding how the meaning of language is conveyed through its structure.

Applications of Syntax and Semantics:

Syntax and semantics are used in a wide variety of natural language processing applications. In machine translation, syntax and semantics are used to generate grammatically correct and semantically appropriate translations.

In sentiment analysis, syntax and semantics are used to understand the emotional content of sentences. In text classification, syntax and semantics are used to identify the topic of a document.

Syntax and semantics are two fundamental concepts in natural language processing. Syntax is concerned with the structure and organization of sentences, while semantics is concerned with the meaning of sentences. The interface between syntax and semantics is an important area of study in natural language processing.

By leveraging syntax and semantics, ChatGPT models can generate responses that are not only grammatically correct but also semantically appropriate to the context and intent of the conversation.

By understanding these concepts, organizations can build ChatGPT models that are better equipped to handle the nuances and complexities of human language.

By leveraging techniques such as language modeling, semantic representation, and discourse analysis, organizations can build ChatGPT models that are capable of generating responses that are contextually appropriate, semantically relevant, and grammatically correct.

Multi-Modal NLP Techniques
Such As Image Captioning And Speech Recognition

Multi-modal NLP refers to the integration of multiple modalities, such as text, images, and speech, in natural language processing. Multi-modal NLP techniques aim to capture the complex relationships between different modalities and generate more accurate and meaningful results.

Two important multi-modal NLP techniques are image captioning and speech recognition.

Image Captioning:

Image captioning is a task that involves generating natural language descriptions of images.

Image captioning is a multi-modal NLP technique because it requires the integration of visual information from images with the language modeling capabilities of natural language processing.

Image captioning models typically use convolutional neural networks (CNNs) to extract visual features from images and recurrent neural networks (RNNs) to generate natural language descriptions.

Image captioning is a task in which an algorithm generates a natural language description of an image.

The goal is to accurately and concisely describe the content of the image in a way that a human could understand. Image captioning is a challenging problem, as it requires both computer vision and natural language processing techniques to work together effectively.

Image Feature Extraction:
The first step in image captioning is to extract features from the image. This involves converting the raw pixel values of the image into a set of features that can be used for language modeling.

One popular approach is to use a convolutional neural network (CNN) to extract features from the image. The CNN takes the image as input and outputs a set of high-level features that capture the content of the image.

Language Modeling:
Once the image features have been extracted, the next step is to generate a natural language description of the image. This is typically done using a recurrent neural network (RNN) or a transformer model, which takes the image features as input and generates a sequence of words that describe the image.

The RNN or transformer model is trained on a large corpus of captioned images to learn the relationships between image features and language.

Evaluation:
There are several metrics used to evaluate the performance of an image captioning model. One common metric is BLEU (Bilingual Evaluation Understudy), which measures the similarity between the generated caption and a set of reference captions.

Another metric is METEOR (Metric for Evaluation of Translation with Explicit ORdering), which takes into account the ordering of words in the generated caption and the reference captions.

Applications:
Image captioning has several practical applications. For example, it can be used to provide descriptions of images for visually impaired individuals, or to automatically caption images in social media feeds.

Image captioning can also be used in robotics, where a robot needs to be able to understand the content of an image in order to perform a task.

Challenges:
Image captioning is a challenging task, as it requires both computer vision and natural language processing techniques to work together effectively.

One challenge is the variability and ambiguity inherent in natural language, which can make it difficult to generate accurate and concise captions. Another challenge is the need for large amounts of training data, as well as computational resources to train and deploy the model.

Image captioning is an important task in natural language processing and computer vision, with many practical applications. By leveraging image features extracted from a convolutional neural network and natural language modeling techniques, image captioning models can generate accurate and meaningful descriptions of images.

However, there are still many challenges to be addressed in image captioning, including the need for large amounts of training data and the need to handle the variability and ambiguity inherent in natural language.

Speech Recognition:

Speech recognition is a task that involves converting spoken language into text. Speech recognition is a multi-modal NLP technique because it requires the integration of acoustic information from speech signals with the language modeling capabilities of natural language processing.

Speech recognition models typically use deep neural networks (DNNs) to extract acoustic features from speech signals and generate text transcripts.

Speech recognition, also known as automatic speech recognition (ASR), is a technology that allows a computer to transcribe spoken language into text. Speech recognition is a challenging task, as it requires the system to accurately recognize and interpret the nuances of human speech.

Acoustic Modeling:
The first step in speech recognition is to convert the audio input into a sequence of acoustic features. This is typically done using a technique called spectrogram analysis, which transforms the audio signal into a visual representation of the frequency content over time.

The resulting spectrogram is then fed into an acoustic model, which is typically a deep neural network (DNN) that has been trained on a large corpus of audio data to recognize phonemes and other speech units.

Language Modeling:

Once the audio input has been converted into a sequence of phonemes and other speech units, the next step is to generate a natural language transcription of the spoken words.

This is typically done using a language model, which is a statistical model that estimates the probability of different word sequences given the acoustic features. The language model is trained on a large corpus of transcribed speech data to learn the relationships between acoustic features and language.

Decoding:

The final step in speech recognition is to decode the acoustic features and language model probabilities into a sequence of words that represents the spoken input.

This is typically done using a decoder algorithm that searches through the possible word sequences and selects the most likely sequence based on the acoustic and language model probabilities.

Evaluation:

There are several metrics used to evaluate the performance of a speech recognition system. One common metric is word error rate (WER), which measures the percentage of words in the transcription that are incorrect. Another metric is phoneme error rate (PER), which measures the percentage of phonemes in the transcription that are incorrect.

Applications:

Speech recognition has many practical applications, including voice assistants, transcription services, and dictation software. Speech recognition can also be used in healthcare to transcribe patient notes and in call centers to transcribe customer service conversations.

Challenges:
Speech recognition is a challenging task, as it requires the system to accurately recognize and interpret the nuances of human speech.

One challenge is the variability and ambiguity inherent in natural language, which can make it difficult to accurately transcribe spoken words. Another challenge is the need for large amounts of training data, as well as computational resources to train and deploy the model.

Speech recognition is an important task in natural language processing, with many practical applications. By leveraging acoustic modeling, language modeling, and decoding algorithms, speech recognition systems can accurately transcribe spoken language into text.

However, there are still many challenges to be addressed in speech recognition, including the need for large amounts of training data and the need to handle the variability and ambiguity inherent in natural language.

Some Applications of Multi-Modal NLP:

Multi-modal NLP techniques have a wide range of applications. In image captioning, multi-modal NLP techniques can be used to generate natural language descriptions of images for visually impaired individuals or to improve the accessibility of visual content.

In speech recognition, multi-modal NLP techniques can be used to improve the accuracy of speech-to-text transcription in noisy environments or for non-native speakers.

Multi-modal NLP, also known as multi-modal natural language processing, is a field that combines natural language processing (NLP) with other modalities such as images, videos, and audio.

By integrating multiple modalities, multi-modal NLP can improve the performance of various NLP tasks, such as language understanding and generation.

Applications of Multi-Modal NLP:

There are many applications of multi-modal NLP across various industries. Here are some examples:

Image Captioning:
One popular application of multi-modal NLP is image captioning, which involves generating natural language descriptions of images. This is useful for applications such as search engines, where users can search for images using natural language queries.

Speech Recognition:
As discussed earlier, speech recognition is an important application of multi-modal NLP. By combining audio input with natural language processing, speech recognition systems can accurately transcribe spoken language into text.

Sentiment Analysis:
Sentiment analysis is the task of identifying the sentiment expressed in a text, such as positive, negative, or neutral. By combining text with other modalities such as images or audio, multi-modal NLP can improve the accuracy of sentiment analysis by capturing additional contextual information.

Text-to-Speech:
Text-to-speech (TTS) is the task of converting written text into spoken language. By combining natural language processing with audio processing, multi-modal NLP can generate more natural-sounding speech that is better suited for applications such as voice assistants and audiobooks.

Machine Translation:
Machine translation is the task of translating text from one language to another. By integrating visual cues such as images or videos, multi-modal NLP can improve the accuracy of machine translation by providing additional contextual information that is not available in the text alone.

Challenges:
While multi-modal NLP has many potential applications, there are also many challenges to be addressed. One challenge is the need for large amounts of training data that includes multiple modalities. Another challenge is the need for specialized models that can handle multiple modalities and integrate them effectively.

Multi-modal NLP is an exciting field with many potential applications across various industries. By combining natural language processing with other modalities such as images, videos, and audio, multi-modal NLP can improve the performance of various NLP tasks.

However, there are still many challenges to be addressed in multi-modal NLP, such as the need for large amounts of training data and specialized models.

The Challenges in Multi-Modal NLP

Multi-modal NLP techniques face several challenges. One challenge is the lack of large-scale multi-modal datasets that capture the complex relationships between different modalities.

Another challenge is the integration of different modalities in a meaningful way, as different modalities may have different levels of importance or contribute differently to the overall meaning of a message. Finally, multi-modal NLP techniques must be able to handle the variability and ambiguity inherent in natural language.

Multi-modal NLP is a rapidly growing field that combines natural language processing (NLP) with other modalities such as images, videos, and audio. While multi-modal NLP has many potential applications, there are also many challenges to be addressed.

Challenges of Multi-Modal NLP:

Data Collection:
One of the biggest challenges in multi-modal NLP is data collection. Collecting large amounts of data that includes multiple modalities can be difficult and time-consuming. Additionally, different modalities may require different annotation methods, which can further complicate the data collection process.

Integration:
Integrating multiple modalities effectively is another challenge in multi-modal NLP. Different modalities may provide complementary or conflicting information, and it can be difficult to decide how to integrate this information effectively. Additionally, different modalities may require different preprocessing and feature extraction methods, which can further complicate the integration process.

Model Complexity:
Multi-modal NLP models can be more complex than traditional NLP models due to the need to handle multiple modalities. This can make training and optimization more difficult, and may require specialized hardware or software to handle the increased computational requirements.

Evaluation:
Evaluating the performance of multi-modal NLP models can be challenging. Traditional NLP evaluation metrics may not be sufficient for evaluating multi-modal models, and new evaluation metrics may need to be developed. Additionally, the lack of standardized benchmarks for multi-modal NLP can make it difficult to compare the performance of different models.

Domain Adaptation:
Multi-modal NLP models may perform differently in different domains or on different types of data. Domain adaptation techniques may be necessary to adapt models trained on one domain to perform well on another domain. However, domain adaptation can be challenging, particularly when dealing with multiple modalities.

Multi-modal NLP is a challenging but promising field with many potential applications. Addressing the challenges in multi-modal NLP will require a combination of technical expertise, data collection and annotation, and innovative evaluation methods.

By overcoming these challenges, multi-modal NLP has the potential to revolutionize natural language processing and enable new applications in areas such as image captioning, speech recognition, and sentiment analysis.

Multi-modal NLP techniques, such as image captioning and speech recognition, are important for capturing the complex relationships between different modalities and generating more accurate and meaningful results.

By leveraging multi-modal NLP techniques, ChatGPT models can generate responses that are not only linguistically accurate but also take into account visual or auditory cues, improving the overall quality and relevance of the conversation.

However, there are still many challenges to be addressed in multi-modal NLP, including the lack of large-scale datasets and the need for more sophisticated integration techniques.

Neural Machine Translation (NMT)
and its Variations

Neural Machine Translation (NMT) is a type of machine translation that uses neural networks to translate text from one language to another.

Compared to traditional machine translation approaches, NMT has achieved state-of-the-art performance on many language pairs. However, there are also several variations of NMT that have been proposed to address some of its limitations.

Basic NMT Model:

The basic NMT model consists of an encoder network that converts the source language sentence into a fixed-length vector representation, and a decoder network that generates the target language sentence from the encoder output.

Both the encoder and decoder networks are typically implemented using recurrent neural networks (RNNs) or more recently, transformer networks.

The basic NMT model suffers from the problem of vanishing gradients, where the gradients can become very small during backpropagation, which can make it difficult to train the model effectively.

Variations of NMT:

Attention Mechanism:

The attention mechanism was introduced to address the problem of vanishing gradients in NMT. The attention mechanism allows the decoder network to selectively attend to different parts of the encoder output, instead of relying solely on the fixed-length vector representation. This can improve the performance of NMT and reduce the problem of vanishing gradients.

Multi-Source NMT:

Multi-source NMT is an extension of NMT that allows the model to translate from multiple source languages to a single target language. This can be useful in scenarios where there are multiple source languages that need to be translated into the same target language, such as in the European Union.

Multi-Task NMT:

Multi-task NMT is another extension of NMT that allows the model to perform multiple tasks simultaneously, such as translating between multiple language pairs or performing both translation and text summarization. This can improve the efficiency of the model and enable it to learn more from the available data.

Unsupervised NMT:

Unsupervised NMT is a variation of NMT that does not require parallel corpora for training. Instead, it uses unsupervised learning techniques such as back-translation and language modeling to train the model. Unsupervised NMT has the potential to make machine translation accessible to low-resource languages and enable machine translation in wscenarios where parallel corpora are not available.

NMT and its variations have made significant progress in machine translation, achieving state-of-the-art performance on many language pairs.

However, there are still many challenges to be addressed, such as domain adaptation, low-resource language translation, and incorporating external knowledge into the model.

By addressing these challenges, NMT and its variations have the potential to revolutionize machine translation and make it more accessible and effective for a wider range of languages and applications.

CHAPTER 3
ADVANCED
A. I. N.L.P. PROMPT MASTER
ENGINEERING

Chapter 3 focuses on advanced engineering techniques for ChatGPT Prompt Masters. These techniques are critical for achieving state-of-the-art performance and scaling ChatGPT Prompt models to handle large amounts of data and users.

Model Optimization:
Model optimization involves improving the efficiency and performance of the ChatGPT Prompt model by reducing its computational requirements while maintaining its accuracy. This can be achieved through techniques such as pruning, quantization, and knowledge distillation.

Pruning involves removing unimportant weights from the model, while quantization reduces the precision of the model's parameters. Knowledge distillation involves training a smaller "student" model to mimic the behavior of a larger "teacher" model, which can also help reduce the model's computational requirements.

Parallelization:
Parallelization involves distributing the workload of the ChatGPT Prompt model across multiple computing resources, such as multiple GPUs or CPUs. This can improve the efficiency of the model and enable it to handle larger amounts of data and users.

Parallelization can be achieved through techniques such as data parallelism, model parallelism, and pipeline parallelism. Data parallelism involves splitting the input data across multiple GPUs or CPUs and computing the model's output in parallel. Model parallelism involves splitting the model across multiple GPUs or CPUs and computing different parts of the model in parallel. Pipeline parallelism involves splitting the model into stages and computing each stage in parallel.

Deployment:

Deployment involves integrating the ChatGPT Prompt model into a production environment, such as a web or mobile application, and ensuring that it can handle the expected workload and traffic.

This can involve optimizing the model's inference speed, minimizing its memory requirements, and ensuring that it can handle errors and failures gracefully. Deployment can also involve monitoring the model's performance and making adjustments as necessary.

Advanced engineering techniques such as model optimization, parallelization, and deployment are critical for achieving state-of-the-art performance and scaling ChatGPT Prompt models to handle large amounts of data and users.

By implementing these techniques, ChatGPT Prompt Masters can improve the efficiency and accuracy of their models and make them more accessible and effective for a wider range of applications and users.

How To Build And Fine-Tune
State-Of-The-Art Chatgpt Models

Building and fine-tuning state-of-the-art ChatGPT models requires a deep understanding of natural language processing (NLP) concepts and techniques, as well as expertise in machine learning and model development.

In this section, we'll explore the key steps involved in building and fine-tuning a ChatGPT model, from data preparation and model architecture to hyperparameter tuning and evaluation.

Data Preparation:
The first step in building a ChatGPT model is to prepare the training data. This involves selecting and cleaning the data, as well as preprocessing it for use with the model.

Depending on the application, the data may need to be labeled or annotated with additional information, such as part-of-speech tags or named entities.

Model Architecture:
The architecture of the ChatGPT model plays a critical role in its performance and accuracy. There are several different types of architectures that can be used for ChatGPT models, including transformer-based architectures like GPT-3 or more traditional recurrent neural network (RNN) architectures.

The choice of architecture will depend on the specific requirements of the application and the characteristics of the training data.

Fine-Tuning:
Once the architecture of the ChatGPT model has been selected, the next step is to fine-tune it on the specific task or dataset at hand. Fine-tuning involves adjusting the model's parameters and hyperparameters to optimize its performance on the specific task or dataset.

This can involve adjusting the learning rate, batch size, or regularization parameters, as well as experimenting with different optimization algorithms or weight initialization schemes.

Hyperparameter Tuning:

Hyperparameter tuning is the process of selecting the optimal values for the hyperparameters of the ChatGPT model, such as the number of layers, hidden size, and number of attention heads.

This can be done through manual tuning or using automated techniques such as grid search or random search. Hyperparameter tuning is a critical step in building a state-of-the-art ChatGPT model, as it can significantly impact the model's performance and accuracy.

Evaluation:

The final step in building a state-of-the-art ChatGPT model is to evaluate its performance on a held-out test set or in a real-world application. This involves measuring the model's accuracy, speed, and efficiency, as well as assessing its ability to handle different types of input and output.

Evaluation is an ongoing process, and models may need to be retrained or fine-tuned based on new data or feedback from users.

Building and fine-tuning state-of-the-art ChatGPT models requires a deep understanding of NLP concepts and techniques, as well as expertise in machine learning and model development.

By following the key steps outlined above, developers and researchers can build models that are optimized for their specific task or application and achieve state-of-the-art performance and accuracy.

However, building state-of-the-art models also requires careful consideration of factors such as computational resources, data quality, and model interpretability, and may require collaboration with experts in other fields such as linguistics or cognitive science.

Leveraging External Data Sources To Improve
The Quality Of Generated Text

One of the key challenges in natural language generation tasks such as ChatGPT is the need to produce text that is not only coherent and grammatically correct, but also relevant and informative. One way to achieve this is to leverage external data sources to improve the quality of generated text.

There are several approaches to incorporating external data sources into ChatGPT models. One common approach is to use pre-trained language models such as BERT or GPT-2 to fine-tune the model on a specific domain or task. For example, if the goal is to generate text about a specific topic, the model can be fine-tuned on a corpus of text related to that topic to improve its ability to generate relevant and informative text.

Another approach is to use knowledge graphs or ontologies to provide structured knowledge about a specific domain or topic. This can help the model generate more accurate and informative text by enabling it to make connections between different concepts and pieces of information.

Yet another approach is to use external data sources such as news articles, social media posts, or scientific publications to provide additional context or information that can help the model generate more relevant and informative text. This can be particularly useful in domains where there is a large amount of unstructured data available, such as social media or news articles.

However, there are also challenges associated with leveraging external data sources in ChatGPT models. One major challenge is the need to ensure that the data is of high quality and relevant to the task at hand. This requires careful selection and curation of the data, as well as ongoing monitoring and evaluation to ensure that the model is generating high-quality text.

Another challenge is the potential for bias or misinformation in the external data sources. This can be particularly problematic in domains such as news or social media, where there is a risk of propagating false or misleading information.

Leveraging external data sources can be a powerful tool for improving the quality of generated text in ChatGPT models, but it requires careful consideration of the trade-offs and challenges involved.

Let's consider some examples of how external data sources can be used to improve the quality of generated text in ChatGPT models.

First, let's consider the use of pre-trained language models to fine-tune ChatGPT models for specific tasks or domains. For example, suppose we want to generate text about the weather.

We could fine-tune a ChatGPT model on a large corpus of weather-related text, such as weather reports or meteorological data, to improve its ability to generate accurate and informative text about the weather.

Similarly, we could use pre-trained language models to fine-tune ChatGPT models for other specific domains or tasks, such as legal document generation or customer service chatbots. By fine-tuning the model on a relevant corpus of text, we can improve its ability to generate text that is both relevant and informative for the specific domain or task.

Another example of leveraging external data sources is the use of knowledge graphs or ontologies. For example, suppose we want to generate text about a particular disease. We could use a knowledge graph or ontology to provide structured information about the disease, such as its symptoms, causes, and treatments. This can help the model generate more accurate and informative text by enabling it to make connections between different pieces of information and generate text that is more coherent and relevant.

Let's consider the use of external data sources such as news articles or social media posts to provide additional context or information. For example, suppose we want to generate text about a particular news event, such as a natural disaster or political crisis. We could use external data sources such as news articles or social media posts to provide additional context or information that can help the model generate more relevant and informative text.

Here are 10 more examples of how external data sources can be used to improve the quality of generated text in ChatGPT models:

1. Using knowledge bases, such as Wikipedia or Wikidata, to provide additional information or context for generating text on a wide range of topics.

2. Leveraging sentiment analysis models to improve the tone and sentiment of generated text in customer service chatbots or social media bots.

3. Incorporating knowledge of slang and informal language through external data sources such as online forums or chat rooms to improve the naturalness and fluency of generated text.

4. Using external data sources such as product reviews or customer feedback to train ChatGPT models for generating product descriptions or advertisements.

5. Leveraging domain-specific ontologies or taxonomies to improve the accuracy and relevance of generated text in specialized domains such as medicine or finance.

6. Using external data sources such as news articles or historical documents to provide historical context for generating text on historical events or figures.

7. Incorporating user feedback or ratings to train ChatGPT models for generating personalized recommendations or suggestions.

8. Using external data sources such as online dictionaries or thesauri to improve the vocabulary and word choice of generated text.

9. Leveraging multimodal data sources, such as images or videos, to generate descriptive or captioned text.

10. Using external data sources such as social media posts or customer reviews to generate text that is tailored to the preferences and interests of specific target audiences.

However, there are also challenges associated with these approaches. For example, ensuring that the data is of high quality and relevant to the task at hand can be difficult.

Additionally, there is a risk of bias or misinformation in the external data sources, particularly in domains such as news or social media where there is a risk of propagating false or misleading information.

Therefore, it is important to carefully select and curate the external data sources used in ChatGPT models and to continuously monitor and evaluate the quality of the generated text.

Managing Large-Scale Model Training
With Distributed Computing

As the size and complexity of ChatGPT models continue to increase, training these models on a single machine becomes increasingly impractical. This is where distributed computing comes into play.

Distributed computing involves splitting the computational workload across multiple machines, or nodes, in a network, allowing for much faster and more efficient model training. In the context of ChatGPT models, distributed computing can be used to train models using massive amounts of data and parameters, resulting in more accurate and sophisticated models.

There are several distributed computing frameworks that can be used for managing large-scale model training, including TensorFlow, PyTorch, and Horovod. These frameworks allow for the efficient distribution of data and computations across multiple nodes, as well as the ability to scale up or down the number of nodes as needed.

One important consideration when using distributed computing for model training is data sharding, which involves partitioning the training data into smaller chunks and distributing them across multiple nodes. This helps to reduce the amount of data that needs to be stored on each node, and also reduces the amount of data that needs to be transferred between nodes during training.

Another important aspect of managing large-scale model training is monitoring and debugging. With distributed computing, it can be more difficult to identify and fix errors, since they may be occurring on different nodes or at different stages of the training process. Therefore, it is important to have effective monitoring and debugging tools in place to quickly identify and resolve any issues that arise.

Managing large-scale model training with distributed computing is an important aspect of building state-of-the-art ChatGPT models. By leveraging the power of distributed computing, researchers and engineers can train larger and more complex models, resulting in improved performance and more accurate text generation.

Here are some additional details and examples to illustrate the importance and practical applications of managing large-scale model training with distributed computing:

One key advantage of distributed computing is its ability to handle large amounts of data.

For example, in natural language processing, models trained on large-scale datasets such as the Common Crawl corpus, which contains billions of web pages, can provide significant improvements in language understanding and text generation.

In addition to handling large datasets, distributed computing can also be used to train models with a large number of parameters. For example, the GPT-3 model, which has over 175 billion parameters, requires significant computational resources to train.

By distributing the training workload across multiple nodes, researchers can more efficiently train such large-scale models.

Distributed computing is also critical for training models in real-world production environments.

For example, in chatbots or virtual assistants, the models need to be trained on a continuous stream of user queries and feedback. With distributed computing, the training workload can be distributed across multiple nodes, allowing for continuous and efficient model training.

Another example of the importance of distributed computing is in the field of image recognition.

For example, models like ResNet and InceptionV3, which are commonly used for image classification tasks, have millions of parameters, and require large amounts of data to be trained effectively.

By using distributed computing frameworks like TensorFlow or PyTorch, researchers can more efficiently train these models on large-scale datasets.

One challenge of distributed computing is ensuring that the nodes are communicating effectively and efficiently. One way to address this challenge is by using specialized hardware, such as GPUs or TPUs, which are designed to handle the specific requirements of deep learning models.

By using specialized hardware, researchers can ensure that the nodes are communicating efficiently and that the training process is optimized for performance.

Managing large-scale model training with distributed computing is critical for building state-of-the-art ChatGPT models.

By leveraging the power of distributed computing, researchers and engineers can handle large-scale datasets, train models with a large number of parameters, and efficiently train models in real-world production environments.

While there are challenges associated with distributed computing, such as ensuring effective communication between nodes, the benefits of using this approach for model training are clear.

CHAPTER 4
ADVANCED TECHNIQUES
FOR TEXT GENERATION

In this chapter, we'll explore advanced techniques for generating text using ChatGPT models. We'll delve into several state-of-the-art approaches that have been developed to improve the quality, diversity, and coherence of generated text.

We'll cover is fine-tuning GPT models for specific text generation tasks. This involves training the model on a specific dataset and task, such as summarization or translation, to improve its performance on that particular task. We'll also discuss techniques for using pre-trained models, such as GPT-3, to generate high-quality text with minimal fine-tuning.

We will cover is how to generate more diverse and interesting text. We'll explore techniques such as top-k sampling, nucleus sampling, and temperature sampling, which allow the model to generate a wider range of outputs while still maintaining coherence and quality.

We'll also discuss methods for controlling the content and style of generated text. This includes techniques such as conditional generation, where the model is conditioned on a specific input, such as a topic or sentiment, to generate text that aligns with that input.

We'll also discuss techniques for style transfer, where the model can generate text in different styles, such as formal or casual, based on a given prompt.

Furthermore, we'll dive into how to generate long-form text, such as essays or articles. This includes techniques such as hierarchical generation, where the model generates text in sections or paragraphs, and text planning, where the model first generates an outline or structure for the text before filling in the details.

This chapter will provide advanced techniques for generating high-quality, diverse, and controlled text using ChatGPT models.

Adapting to Diverse Text Generation Tasks
such as Question-Answering, Storytelling, and Content Creation

As a ChatGPT Prompt Master, it is important to be able to adapt to diverse text generation tasks. Some examples of such tasks include question-answering, storytelling, and content creation.

Question-answering involves generating a response to a specific question based on a given context. This requires the model to understand the context and extract relevant information to generate an accurate response. For example, a question like "What is the capital of France?" can be answered by generating the response "Paris".

Question-Answering (QA) is a task where a machine is given a question in natural language and is expected to provide an answer in natural language as well. This task is crucial for various applications such as customer service chatbots, search engines, and personal assistants.

To perform QA, the machine needs to understand the question and retrieve the relevant information from a given knowledge source, such as a database or a large corpus of text. The retrieved information is then used to generate the answer.

There are various approaches to perform QA, such as rule-based, template-based, and machine learning-based methods. Machine learning-based methods, particularly deep learning techniques, have shown promising results in recent years.

One example of a machine learning-based QA model is the BERT (Bidirectional Encoder Representations from Transformers) model.

BERT is a pre-trained language model that can be fine-tuned for various NLP tasks, including QA. In the fine-tuning process, the model is trained on a specific QA dataset, where the input is a question and the output is the corresponding answer.

For instance, consider the following question: "What is the capital of France?" The BERT model can retrieve the answer "Paris" by understanding the question and retrieving the relevant information from a knowledge source such as a database or a corpus of text.

Another example of a QA model is the open-domain QA model. This model is designed to answer a wide range of questions from various domains, without relying on a specific knowledge source. The model generates the answer by using a large corpus of text, such as Wikipedia.

For example, a user might ask "Who invented the telephone?" The open-domain QA model would generate an answer by extracting relevant information from a large corpus of text, such as Wikipedia, and returning the answer "Alexander Graham Bell."

QA is an essential task in NLP, and there are various approaches and models available to perform this task. The choice of model depends on the specific requirements of the application, and the availability of a suitable knowledge source.

Storytelling involves generating a coherent and engaging story based on a given prompt or topic. This requires the model to have a strong understanding of narrative structure and character development, as well as the ability to generate descriptive and engaging language.

For example, a prompt like "Write a story about a young girl who discovers she has magical powers" can be used to generate a compelling story that captures the reader's attention.

Storytelling is one of the diverse text generation tasks that a ChatGPT Prompt Master can adapt to. It involves generating a coherent and engaging story with a clear plot, characters, and setting.

One approach to generating stories is to use a prompt that sets the tone, setting, and characters of the story, and then use the model to generate the rest of the story. For example, given the prompt "A detective investigates a mysterious murder in a small town", the model can generate a story with twists and turns that keeps the reader engaged.

Here's an example of a generated story using this approach:

Detective Johnson arrived in the small town of Maplewood, where a mysterious murder had taken place. He walked through the quiet streets, taking in the quaint houses and the suspicious glances of the townspeople. He knew that he had to tread carefully if he wanted to solve the case.

As he questioned the locals, he discovered that the victim was a well-known businessman who had many enemies. He also found out that the victim had a secret affair with a young woman who lived on the outskirts of town.

The detective went to visit the woman, hoping that she would give him some insight into the victim's life. But when he arrived, he found her dead, with the same mysterious markings on her body as the previous victim.

As the detective delved deeper into the case, he uncovered a web of lies and deceit that led him to the real killer. It was the victim's business partner, who had been embezzling money and feared being exposed.

Another approach to generating stories is to use a style transfer technique, where the model is trained to mimic the style of a particular author or genre.

For example, given the prompt "Write a horror story in the style of Stephen King", the model can generate a story that feels like it was written by the famous horror author.

Here's an example of a generated horror story in the style of Stephen King:

The old house on the edge of town had always been rumored to be haunted. But when a group of teenagers dared to explore its dusty halls, they discovered something far more terrifying than any ghost.

As they descended into the basement, the air grew colder and the shadows grew longer. They heard strange whispers and felt unseen hands brushing against their skin. And then they saw it - a creature that defied description, with writhing tentacles and glowing red eyes.

They tried to run, but the creature was too fast. It cornered them in a small room, where they huddled together in terror. And then it began to speak, in a voice that sounded like the scraping of nails on a chalkboard.

"I have been waiting for you," it said. "You are the sacrifice I need to break the curse that has kept me trapped in this house for centuries."

The teenagers tried to fight back, but their efforts were futile. One by one, they were consumed by the creature, until only one remained. And as she watched her friends being devoured, she knew that she would never escape the horror that lurked within the old house on the edge of town.

In both of these examples, the ChatGPT Prompt Master leverages advanced text generation techniques to create engaging and immersive stories that captivate the reader.

Here are a few more examples of storytelling using advanced text generation techniques:

Automated screenwriting:
ChatGPT can be trained on large datasets of screenplays to generate new scripts for movies or television shows. These scripts can be used as a starting point for human screenwriters to refine and develop.

Virtual Storybook:
ChatGPT can be used to generate interactive stories for children's books. By incorporating natural language processing and machine learning, the stories can be tailored to the child's interests and reading level.

Personalized News Articles:
ChatGPT can generate news articles based on a user's interests and preferences. This allows for highly targeted and relevant content to be delivered to the user, improving their overall experience and engagement.

Creative Writing Assistance:
ChatGPT can be used to assist human writers in developing their own stories or novels. By providing suggestions and prompts, ChatGPT can help writers overcome writer's block and generate new ideas.

Fanfiction Generation:
ChatGPT can be trained on existing fanfiction to generate new stories in the same universe or with the same characters. This allows fans to continue to explore their favorite fictional worlds even after the original creator has stopped producing content.

Content creation involves generating high-quality content for a specific purpose, such as product descriptions, blog articles, or social media posts. This requires the model to have a strong understanding of the intended audience and the purpose of the content, as well as the ability to generate persuasive and engaging language.

For example, a prompt like "Write a product description for a new line of running shoes" can be used to generate a compelling description that highlights the features and benefits of the product.

Content creation is one of the most important applications of text generation. In this context, content refers to any kind of written material that can be used for various purposes such as marketing, education, entertainment, and more.

With the help of advanced text generation techniques, it is now possible to create high-quality content with minimal human involvement.

One of the key challenges in content creation is to ensure that the generated text is engaging and informative. This requires a deep understanding of the target audience and the type of content that they are looking for.

For instance, a marketing copy for a fashion brand would require a different tone and style compared to a technical whitepaper for a software company.

Another challenge is to maintain consistency and coherence throughout the text. This is especially important for longer pieces of content such as articles and essays.

In order to achieve this, the generated text must have a clear structure and flow, with each paragraph and sentence building upon the previous ones.

Here are some examples of content that can be created with the help of text generation:

Blog Post Generation:
ChatGPT models can generate high-quality blog posts on any topic.

For instance, if the input prompt is "Write a blog post on the benefits of meditation", the model can generate a comprehensive blog post with relevant information and sources.

Product Descriptions:
E-commerce websites can use ChatGPT models to generate compelling product descriptions. For instance, if the input prompt is "Write a product description for a coffee machine", the model can generate a detailed and persuasive description of the product.

Marketing Copy:
ChatGPT models can generate marketing copy for various purposes, such as social media posts, email newsletters, and landing pages.

For example, if the input prompt is "Write a social media post for a new skincare product", the model can generate an engaging post with relevant hashtags and product features.

Video Scripts:
ChatGPT models can generate scripts for various types of videos, such as explainer videos, product demos, and tutorials.

For instance, if the input prompt is "Write a script for a cooking tutorial video", the model can generate a step-by-step guide with detailed instructions.

Creative Writing:
ChatGPT models can be used to generate creative writing pieces, such as short stories, poems, and screenplays.

For example, if the input prompt is "Write a short story about a detective solving a murder case", the model can generate a compelling story with plot twists and interesting characters.

News Articles:
ChatGPT models can generate news articles on various topics, such as politics, sports, and entertainment.

For instance, if the input prompt is "Write a news article on the impact of climate change on wildlife", the model can generate a well-researched and informative article.

Technical Writing:
ChatGPT models can generate technical writing pieces, such as user manuals, API documentation, and research papers.

For example, if the input prompt is "Write a user manual for a mobile app", the model can generate a clear and concise guide with screenshots and step-by-step instructions.

Email Templates:
ChatGPT models can generate email templates for various purposes, such as customer support, sales, and marketing.

For instance, if the input prompt is "Write an email template for a follow-up sales email", the model can generate a personalized email with a call-to-action and product benefits.

Social Media Ads:

ChatGPT models can generate ad copy for social media platforms, such as Facebook, Instagram, and Twitter.

For example, if the input prompt is "Write ad copy for a new gym membership offer", the model can generate an eye-catching and persuasive ad with a discount code and promotional offer.

Academic Writing:

ChatGPT models can generate academic writing pieces, such as essays, research papers, and literature reviews.
For instance, if the input prompt is "Write a research paper on the impact of social media on mental health", the model can generate a well-structured and informative paper with relevant studies and citations.

Social Media Captions:

ChatGPT models can be fine-tuned to generate captions for social media platforms such as Instagram, Facebook, or Twitter. These captions can be optimized for engagement and can help social media marketers to save time and increase their reach.

Product Descriptions:

E-commerce websites can use ChatGPT models to generate unique and compelling product descriptions for their online stores. This can help businesses to increase their sales and conversion rates.

Email Newsletters:

ChatGPT models can generate personalized email newsletters for businesses to send to their subscribers. These newsletters can be tailored to the interests and preferences of each subscriber, leading to higher open and click-through rates.

Video Scripts:
ChatGPT models can generate scripts for videos, such as explainer videos or product demos. These scripts can be used by businesses to create high-quality video content without the need for expensive video production teams.

Blog Posts:
ChatGPT models can be trained to generate blog posts on a wide range of topics. This can help businesses to produce high-quality content for their websites, improve their SEO, and establish themselves as thought leaders in their industries.

News Articles:
ChatGPT models can be fine-tuned to generate news articles on a wide range of topics. This can help news organizations to produce more content in less time and cover more stories.

Personalized Recommendations:
ChatGPT models can generate personalized recommendations for products, services, or content based on a user's preferences and behavior. This can help businesses to improve customer satisfaction and loyalty.

Creative Writing:
ChatGPT models can generate creative writing such as poetry, short stories, or even entire novels. This can help writers to overcome writer's block and generate new ideas for their work.

Legal Documents:
ChatGPT models can generate legal documents such as contracts or agreements. This can help law firms and legal departments to save time and improve the accuracy of their documents.

Medical Reports:
ChatGPT models can generate medical reports, such as patient histories or discharge summaries. This can help healthcare providers to improve the efficiency and accuracy of their documentation.

Some quicker examples of Text Generation are:

Product descriptions for e-commerce websites

Blog posts on various topics such as health, travel, and finance

Social media posts for promoting products and services.

Email newsletters for subscribers and customers

News articles for online news portals

Educational material such as textbooks and study guides

Video and podcast scripts for content creators

Product manuals and documentation for software and hardware products

Legal documents such as contracts and agreements

Creative writing such as poetry and short stories.

Text generation has the potential to revolutionize the way we create and consume content. By leveraging advanced NLP techniques, we can now generate high-quality text at scale, allowing us to focus on more important tasks such as analysis and decision-making.

Adapting to diverse text generation tasks requires the ChatGPT Prompt Master to have a strong understanding of the specific requirements and nuances of each task, as well as the ability to fine-tune the model to optimize performance for each task.

This may involve adjusting the model architecture, incorporating additional training data, or tuning hyperparameters to optimize performance for the specific task at hand.

Incorporating External Knowledge Sources and Context for Generating More Informative and Coherent Text

In natural language processing, incorporating external knowledge sources and context is critical for generating informative and coherent text.

This is particularly important in situations where the generated text needs to be more than just a simple paraphrase or summary of the input text.

One common approach for incorporating external knowledge sources is to use knowledge graphs, which provide a structured representation of entities and their relationships.

For example, if the input text is a news article about a celebrity, a knowledge graph can be used to provide additional information about the celebrity, such as their age, birthplace, and notable achievements.

Another approach is to use contextual information, such as the current state of the conversation or the user's location, to generate more relevant and informative text.

For example, in a chatbot conversation about restaurants, the bot can use the user's location to provide recommendations for nearby restaurants.

Here are some additional examples of incorporating external knowledge sources and context for generating more informative and coherent text:

In a medical chatbot conversation, incorporating a database of medical terminology and drug interactions to provide more accurate and helpful responses.

In a news article summarization system, incorporating external sources such as social media and blogs to provide a more comprehensive and diverse range of perspectives.

In a legal document generation system, incorporating a database of legal precedents and case law to ensure that the generated document is legally sound and relevant.

In a customer service chatbot, incorporating information about the customer's purchase history to provide personalized and relevant assistance.

In a weather forecasting system, incorporating data from sensors and satellite imagery to generate more accurate and detailed weather reports.

In an educational content generation system, incorporating information about the student's learning level and preferences to generate more engaging and relevant learning materials.

In a language translation system, incorporating external sources such as dictionaries and encyclopedias to ensure that the translation is accurate and comprehensive.

In a financial report generation system, incorporating external data sources such as stock prices and economic indicators to provide more informed and actionable insights.

In a social media sentiment analysis system, incorporating external sources such as news articles and user reviews to provide a more comprehensive analysis of public opinion.

In a marketing copy generation system, incorporating information about the target audience and market trends to generate more effective and persuasive marketing messages.

In a conversational chatbot, incorporating knowledge from a user's previous interactions can help the chatbot understand the user's preferences and tailor its responses accordingly.

In a medical chatbot, incorporating knowledge from medical databases and research papers can help the chatbot provide accurate and up-to-date information about symptoms, treatments, and medications.

In a weather forecasting system, incorporating real-time weather data and historical weather patterns can help the system generate more accurate and informative weather reports.

In a financial news generator, incorporating real-time stock market data and economic indicators can help the system generate more relevant and insightful news articles about the financial markets.

In a recipe generator, incorporating information about a user's dietary preferences and restrictions can help the system generate recipes that are tailored to the user's needs and preferences.

In a travel recommendation system, incorporating information about a user's travel history and preferences can help the system generate more personalized and relevant travel recommendations.

In an educational chatbot, incorporating knowledge from textbooks and educational materials can help the chatbot provide accurate and informative answers to students' questions.

In a news article generator, incorporating information about a reader's location and interests can help the system generate news articles that are relevant and interesting to the reader.

In a customer service chatbot, incorporating information about a customer's previous interactions with the company can help the chatbot provide more personalized and efficient support.

In a social media post generator, incorporating information about trending topics and hashtags can help the system generate posts that are more likely to be seen and shared by users.

Evaluating and Benchmarking the Quality of Generated Text

Evaluating and benchmarking the quality of generated text is a crucial step in the development of ChatGPT models. It involves measuring how well the generated text matches the desired characteristics, such as coherence, informativeness, fluency, and relevance to the prompt.

One common way to evaluate the quality of generated text is to use automated metrics such as perplexity, BLEU, ROUGE, METEOR, and CIDEr.

Perplexity measures how well the model predicts the next word in a sentence given the previous words, while BLEU, ROUGE, METEOR, and CIDEr measure how well the generated text matches the reference text based on n-gram overlap, recall, and precision.

However, automated metrics are not always reliable and may not capture the nuances of human language.

Therefore, it is essential to also perform human evaluation, where humans rate the generated text based on various criteria such as fluency, coherence, relevance, and informativeness. Human evaluation can be done through crowd-sourcing platforms like Amazon Mechanical Turk or by hiring expert annotators.

To benchmark the quality of generated text, researchers often use standard datasets and tasks such as the COCO Captioning Challenge, the ImageNet dataset, or the LAMBADA dataset.

By comparing the performance of different models on the same dataset and task, researchers can assess which model performs best.

It is important to note that evaluating and benchmarking the quality of generated text is an ongoing process as new models and metrics are developed, and the standard datasets and tasks evolve.

Therefore, it is crucial to stay up-to-date with the latest advancements in the field and continuously re-evaluate the quality of generated text.

In addition to evaluating the quality of generated text, it is also important to benchmark and compare different models and techniques.

There are several commonly used metrics for evaluating the quality of generated text, including:

Perplexity: This metric measures how well a language model can predict a sequence of words. A lower perplexity score indicates that the model is better at predicting the next word in a sentence.

BLEU score: The BLEU (Bilingual Evaluation Understudy) score is commonly used to evaluate the quality of machine translation. It measures the overlap between the machine-generated text and a human-generated reference translation.

ROUGE score: The ROUGE (Recall-Oriented Understudy for Gisting Evaluation) score is similar to the BLEU score, but is used for evaluating the quality of summarization and text generation.

Human evaluation: Ultimately, the best way to evaluate the quality of generated text is to have humans read and assess it. Human evaluators can provide valuable insights into the coherence, relevance, and overall quality of the generated text.

It is important to use a combination of these metrics when evaluating and benchmarking the quality of generated text, as no single metric can capture all aspects of text quality.

Additionally, it is important to use appropriate benchmark datasets and ensure that the evaluation process is standardized and reproducible.

By evaluating and benchmarking the quality of generated text, we can identify areas for improvement and continue to advance the state-of-the-art in natural language generation.

Benchmarking is the process of comparing the performance of a model to the performance of other models on a standard dataset.

Benchmark datasets and tasks are commonly used in natural language processing research to compare the performance of different models. Some examples of benchmark datasets include the COCO dataset for image captioning and the SQuAD dataset for question-answering.

In addition to benchmarking, it is important to evaluate the performance of a model on real-world tasks to ensure that the model is useful in practice. Real-world evaluation can involve deploying the model in a production environment and monitoring its performance over time.

Evaluating and benchmarking the quality of generated text is an important step in developing effective natural language processing models.

CHAPTER 5: RESEARCH AND INNOVATION IN CHATGPT PROMPT MASTER

We will now delve into the latest research and innovations in the field of ChatGPT Prompt Master. This chapter will cover topics such as:

Latest developments in deep learning algorithms and architectures for language modeling and text generation.

Emerging techniques for incorporating external knowledge sources and context to improve the quality of generated text.

Innovations in multi-modal NLP techniques, such as image captioning and speech recognition, and their applications.

Advances in evaluating and benchmarking the quality of generated text, including new metrics and techniques for automatic and human evaluation.

Cutting-edge research on neural machine translation (NMT) and its variations, such as unsupervised and semi-supervised learning.

Novel approaches for adapting to diverse text generation tasks, such as question-answering, storytelling, and content creation.

Future directions in ChatGPT Prompt Master research, including the challenges and opportunities that lie ahead.

This chapter will provide a comprehensive overview of the state-of-the-art in ChatGPT Prompt Master research and serve as a resource for researchers and practitioners alike who are interested in advancing the field.

Review of Recent Research Advances in the Field of Text Generation

The field of text generation is constantly evolving and improving, with new research being published on a regular basis. Some recent research advances in the field include:

Pre-Training Techniques:

One of the most notable recent advances in text generation is the use of pre-training techniques, such as GPT-2 and GPT-3 models. These models are pre-trained on massive amounts of text data, allowing them to generate high-quality text that is often indistinguishable from text written by a human.

Multi-Modal Generation:

Another recent advance in text generation is the incorporation of multi-modal data, such as images and audio, into the text generation process. This allows for more dynamic and engaging text that can better convey information and emotions.

Controlled Generation:

Controlled generation is a technique that allows for more precise control over the output of a text generation model. This technique allows the user to specify certain attributes or characteristics of the generated text, such as sentiment, style, or tone.

Adversarial Training:

Adversarial training is a technique that involves training a text generation model in the presence of an adversary, which attempts to trick the model into generating incorrect or misleading text. This technique can help improve the robustness and accuracy of text generation models.

Domain-Specific Generation:

Domain-specific generation involves training a text generation model on a specific domain, such as legal documents or medical records. This can result in more accurate and useful generated text for specific applications.

Multi-Lingual Generation:

Multi-lingual text generation is an emerging field that aims to develop models that can generate high-quality text in multiple languages. This is a challenging task due to the complexities of natural language processing in different languages, but recent advances have shown promising results.

Explainable Generation:

Explainable generation is a technique that aims to provide insight into the decision-making process of text generation models, allowing users to better understand and interpret the generated text. This can help improve the transparency and accountability of text generation models.

The field of text generation is constantly evolving, with new research advances pushing the boundaries of what is possible with text generation models.

As these techniques continue to improve, we can expect to see even more innovative and useful applications of text generation in the future.

Here are some recent research advances in the field of text generation:

GPT-3:

In 2020, OpenAI released GPT-3 (Generative Pre-trained Transformer 3), a large-scale language model with 175 billion parameters. It achieved state-of-the-art performance on various language tasks, including language modeling, machine translation, and text completion.

Few-Shot Learning:

Few-shot learning is a machine learning technique that enables models to learn from a small number of examples. Researchers have used this technique to improve the performance of text generation models on low-resource languages and domains.

Pretraining on Diverse Data Sources:
Recent research has explored pretraining text generation models on diverse data sources, such as images, videos, and audio, to improve their ability to generate informative and creative text.

Controllable Text Generation:
Controllable text generation allows users to specify constraints and preferences for the generated text, such as style, tone, and content. Recent research has developed methods for controllable text generation, such as conditional language models and latent variable models.

Style Transfer:
Style transfer is the process of modifying the style of a given text while preserving its content. Recent research has explored various techniques for style transfer in text generation, such as adversarial training and latent variable models.

Multimodal Text Generation:
Multimodal text generation refers to the generation of text in conjunction with other modalities such as images or videos. Recent research has explored various techniques for multimodal text generation, such as image captioning and video summarization.

Zero-Shot Learning:
Zero-shot learning is a machine learning technique that enables models to generate text for tasks they have not been explicitly trained on. Recent research has explored zero-shot learning in text generation for various tasks, such as question answering and summarization.

> **Evaluation Metrics:**
> As text generation models become more advanced, it becomes increasingly important to develop appropriate evaluation metrics that can accurately measure their performance. Recent research has explored various evaluation metrics for text generation, such as BLEU, ROUGE, and perplexity.

These are just a few examples of recent research advances in the field of text generation. As the field continues to grow and evolve, we can expect to see even more exciting innovations and breakthroughs in the years to come.

Discussion of New and Emerging Techniques in ChatGPT Models

The field of text generation is constantly evolving, and researchers are always exploring new techniques to improve the quality and performance of ChatGPT models.

Here are some of the new and emerging techniques that are currently being explored:

Few-Shot Learning:

Few-shot learning is a technique that allows ChatGPT models to learn from a small amount of data. This is particularly useful in situations where there is limited data available for a specific task, such as in low-resource languages or specialized domains.

With few-shot learning, ChatGPT models can quickly adapt to new tasks with minimal training data.

GAN-Based Text Generation:

Generative Adversarial Networks (GANs) have been widely used in image and video generation, and now researchers are exploring their potential for text generation.

GAN-based text generation involves training two neural networks, a generator and a discriminator, to work together to produce high-quality text that is indistinguishable from human-generated text.

Multi-Task Learning:

Multi-task learning is a technique that involves training a single ChatGPT model to perform multiple related tasks simultaneously.

This can help improve the efficiency and effectiveness of text generation models by allowing them to share knowledge and resources across multiple tasks.

Unsupervised Learning:

Unsupervised learning is a technique that involves training ChatGPT models on large amounts of unlabelled data.

This can help improve the performance of text generation models by allowing them to learn from a wider range of data sources and contexts.

Transfer Learning:

Transfer learning is a technique that involves using pre-trained models to improve the performance of ChatGPT models on new tasks. This can help reduce the amount of training data required for new tasks and improve the efficiency of text generation models.

Attention Mechanisms:

Attention mechanisms are a technique that allows ChatGPT models to selectively focus on different parts of the input sequence when generating text. This can help improve the coherence and fluency of generated text by allowing the model to incorporate context and semantic information more effectively.

Reinforcement Learning:

Reinforcement learning is a technique that involves training ChatGPT models to optimize a specific objective function, such as maximizing the quality or coherence of generated text.

This can help improve the performance of text generation models by allowing them to learn from feedback and adjust their output accordingly.

These new and emerging techniques are helping to advance the field of text generation and improve the quality and performance of ChatGPT models.

As research in this area continues to evolve, we can expect to see even more innovative approaches and techniques being developed.

Opportunities for Innovation
and Improvement in the Field

Opportunities for innovation and improvement in the field of ChatGPT include:

Multilingual ChatGPT:

One opportunity for innovation is to develop ChatGPT models that can generate text in multiple languages. While there have been some advances in multilingual models, there is still room for improvement in terms of accuracy and fluency.

With the increasing need for cross-lingual communication, a ChatGPT model that can generate text in multiple languages can be a valuable tool.

Fine-Tuning On Specific Domains:

Another opportunity for innovation is to develop ChatGPT models that are fine-tuned on specific domains.

For example, a ChatGPT model that is fine-tuned on medical or legal documents can be a valuable tool for professionals in those fields. Fine-tuning on specific domains can also improve the accuracy and fluency of the generated text.

Interactive ChatGPT:

Interactive ChatGPT models that can generate text based on user input can be a valuable tool in various applications, such as virtual assistants or customer service chatbots.

These models can take into account user preferences, history, and context to generate more personalized and relevant responses.

Emotionally-Aware ChatGPT:

Another opportunity for innovation is to develop ChatGPT models that are emotionally-aware. These models can take into account the emotional state of the user and generate text that is more empathetic and supportive.

For example, a ChatGPT model that can detect and respond to the user's emotions can be a valuable tool in mental health applications.

Multi-Modal ChatGPT:

Multi-modal ChatGPT models that can generate text based on multiple sources of information, such as text, images, and audio, can be a valuable tool in various applications, such as video captioning or virtual reality environments.

Explainable ChatGPT:

As ChatGPT models become more complex, it is becoming increasingly important to develop models that can provide explanations for their outputs. Explainable ChatGPT models can help users better understand how the generated text was produced and provide transparency in decision-making processes.

Privacy-Preserving

ChatGPT: Privacy concerns are becoming increasingly important in the development of ChatGPT models. Privacy-preserving ChatGPT models can help to protect the privacy of users by generating text without storing or sharing their personal information.

Domain-Specific Chatgpt Models:

ChatGPT models that are trained specifically for certain domains, such as healthcare or finance, can provide more accurate and relevant responses for specialized use cases.

Adaptive Chatgpt Models:

Models that are able to adapt to individual users and their preferences can provide a more personalized and engaging experience.

Dynamic Chatgpt Models:

Models that are able to dynamically adjust their responses based on real-time changes in the conversation, such as changes in topic or tone, can provide a more natural and human-like experience.

Privacy-Preserving Chatgpt Models:

Techniques such as differential privacy can be used to ensure that sensitive user data is not used to train or generate text with ChatGPT models.

Explainable Chatgpt Models:

Models that are able to provide explanations for their responses can increase trust and understanding of how the model works, which can be important for applications such as customer service.

Hybrid Chatgpt Models:

Combining ChatGPT models with other NLP techniques such as rule-based systems or keyword matching can improve the accuracy and relevance of responses.

Multimodal Chatgpt Models:

Models that can generate text based on multiple modalities, such as text and images, can provide more informative and engaging responses.

Real-Time Chatgpt Models:

Models that are able to generate text in real-time, such as during a live conversation, can be valuable for applications such as live chat customer support.

The opportunities for innovation and improvement in the field of ChatGPT are vast and varied. With the rapid advancements in technology, there is an ever-increasing need for more accurate, personalized, and context-aware text generation.

By exploring new and emerging techniques and developing models that are tailored to specific applications and domains, researchers and practitioners can continue to push the boundaries of what is possible with ChatGPT models.

CHAPTER 6
ETHICS AND SOCIETAL IMPACT
AS AN AI NLP PROMPT MASTER

One important consideration is the potential for biases to be present in the data used to train ChatGPT models. This can result in biased or discriminatory language generation.

For example, if the training data includes predominantly male pronouns in certain contexts, the model may generate text that perpetuates gender biases. To address this, researchers are working on developing methods to detect and remove biases in the training data, as well as strategies for generating unbiased language.

Another issue is the potential for ChatGPT models to be used for malicious purposes, such as generating fake news or propaganda. This can have serious societal implications, as false information can spread quickly and cause harm.

Researchers are exploring ways to detect and prevent the spread of fake information generated by ChatGPT models.

Privacy is also a concern, as ChatGPT models may be trained on sensitive data such as personal emails or medical records. There is a risk that this information could be revealed through generated text. To address this, researchers are developing methods for privacy-preserving training and inference.

There is the issue of accountability for the actions of ChatGPT models. As these models become more sophisticated and powerful, it may be difficult to hold them accountable for harmful or unethical actions. Researchers are exploring ways to make ChatGPT models more transparent and accountable, such as through explainable AI techniques.

Chapter 6 highlights the importance of considering the ethical and societal implications of ChatGPT models, and offers potential solutions to mitigate negative impacts. As ChatGPT technology continues to evolve, it is critical that researchers and practitioners work to ensure that these models are used in a responsible and ethical manner.

Understanding the Ethical Considerations in Building and Deploying Large-Scale Text Generation Models

As the field of natural language processing (NLP) and text generation continues to advance, it is crucial to consider the ethical implications of building and deploying large-scale models such as ChatGPT.

Here are some ethical considerations to keep in mind:

Bias:

Large-scale models are trained on vast amounts of data, which can include biased language. It is important to identify and mitigate biases in both the training data and the generated output.

Misinformation:

Text generation models have the potential to create and disseminate false or misleading information at scale. It is important to ensure that generated text is accurate and trustworthy.

Privacy:

Text generation models often require large amounts of personal data to train effectively. It is important to ensure that user privacy is protected and that data is collected and used in accordance with ethical and legal guidelines.

Accountability:

As text generation models become more powerful and autonomous, it can become difficult to trace responsibility for the actions of these models.

It is important to establish clear lines of accountability and to ensure that those responsible for building and deploying these models are held to ethical standards.

Fairness:

Text generation models have the potential to exacerbate inequalities. It is important to ensure that these models are developed and deployed in ways that are fair and equitable, and that they do not reinforce or perpetuate existing power imbalances.

It is important for researchers, developers, and policymakers to consider the potential ethical implications of text generation models, and to work towards building models that are transparent, accountable, and aligned with ethical principles.

Navigating Potential Societal Impacts
of Generated Text

Generated text, particularly through the use of artificial intelligence (AI) and natural language processing (NLP) technologies, has significant potential to impact society in a number of ways.

As such, it is important to consider and navigate these potential impacts, both positive and negative, as the use of generated text continues to grow and become more prevalent in various industries and contexts.

One potential societal impact of generated text is the perpetuation of bias and discrimination. AI and NLP models are only as unbiased as the data they are trained on, and if the training data contains biases or discriminatory language or concepts, the generated text will likely reflect those biases as well.

Another potential societal impact of generated text is the potential for misinformation and disinformation. With the ability to generate convincing text on a wide range of topics, generated text can be used to spread false or misleading information. This can have significant impacts on public opinion, policy decisions, and other areas of society.

A third potential societal impact of generated text is the potential for harm to individuals or groups. For example, generated text could be used to impersonate someone else, spread false information about them, or otherwise harm their reputation or well-being.

Additionally, generated text could be used to create deepfakes, or realistic synthetic media that can be used to manipulate or deceive people.

Given these potential impacts, it is important for individuals and organizations using generated text to be thoughtful and deliberate in their use and deployment of these technologies.

Being transparent about the use of generated text and the sources of information used to generate it, and engaging in responsible use and dissemination of generated text to avoid spreading misinformation or causing harm.

Additionally, it is important to consider the potential societal impacts of generated text and to develop guidelines to ensure its responsible use. This may involve transparency and accountability in the use of generated text.

While generated text has significant potential to impact society in a variety of ways, it is important to navigate these potential impacts carefully and thoughtfully to ensure that generated text is used in a responsible and beneficial way.

Approaches to Responsible and Transparent Deployment of ChatGPT Models

Deploying ChatGPT models in a responsible and transparent manner is essential to building trust with users and ensuring that the potential impacts of generated text are navigated in a thoughtful and deliberate way. Here are some approaches to responsible and transparent deployment of ChatGPT models:

Addressing Bias and Discrimination:

As mentioned earlier, AI and NLP models are only as unbiased as the data they are trained on. To ensure that ChatGPT models are not perpetuating biases and discrimination, it is important to use representative training data and to evaluate the model's outputs for potential bias or discrimination. Additionally, implement processes for addressing biases or discrimination in the model's outputs.

Providing Transparency and Explanation:

It is important for users to understand how ChatGPT models work and how the generated text is produced. This can be achieved by providing explanations of the model's processes, data sources, and limitations. Additionally, organizations can provide explanations for how the generated text was produced, including details about the inputs and the model's decision-making processes.

Promoting User Privacy and Security:

ChatGPT models may require access to user data to provide personalized responses. To ensure user privacy and security, organizations should implement appropriate security measures, such as encryption and access controls, and obtain user consent for the use of their data.

Mitigating Potential Harm:

As mentioned earlier, generated text has the potential to cause harm, such as spreading misinformation or impersonating individuals. To mitigate these risks, organizations can implement processes for detecting and preventing harmful uses of generated text, such as detecting deepfakes or flagging potentially harmful content.

Engaging in Ethical and Responsible Use:
Organizations deploying ChatGPT models should be aware of the potential societal impacts of generated text and engage in ethical and responsible use of the technology. This can involve developing ethical guidelines and policies for the use of generated text, being transparent about the use of the technology, and engaging in responsible dissemination of generated text.

Deploying ChatGPT models in a responsible and transparent manner involves providing transparency and explanation, promoting user privacy and security, mitigating potential harm, and engaging in ethical and responsible use.

By following these approaches, organizations can build trust with users and ensure that the potential impacts of generated text are navigated in a thoughtful and deliberate way.

CHAPTER 7
INDUSTRY APPLICATIONS OF
CHATGPT PROMPT MASTER

ChatGPT Prompt Master covers the industry applications of this technology.

Here are some possible application topics that may be included:

Customer Service:
ChatGPT models can be used to improve customer service by providing personalized and efficient responses to customer inquiries.

For example, a ChatGPT model can be used to answer frequently asked questions or to provide support for common issues.

Content Generation:
ChatGPT models can be used to generate content for a variety of industries, including journalism, marketing, and entertainment.

For example, a ChatGPT model can be used to generate news articles, product descriptions, or social media posts.

Healthcare:
ChatGPT models can be used to improve healthcare by providing personalized recommendations and assistance.

For example, a ChatGPT model can be used to assist patients in scheduling appointments, providing medication reminders, or answering health-related questions.

Finance:
ChatGPT models can be used in the finance industry to provide personalized financial advice and investment recommendations. For example, a ChatGPT model can be used to provide personalized budgeting advice or to recommend investment opportunities based on a user's financial goals.

Education:

ChatGPT models can be used to provide personalized educational support to students.

For example, a ChatGPT model can be used to provide explanations for complex concepts or to assist students in completing assignments.

Legal Services:

ChatGPT models can be used in the legal industry to provide legal advice and assistance.

For example, a ChatGPT model can be used to provide guidance on legal processes or to answer legal questions.

Human Resources:

ChatGPT models can be used in human resources to assist with recruitment, training, and employee support.

For example, a ChatGPT model can be used to provide information on company policies or to assist with onboarding new employees.

In addition to these industries, there are many other potential applications for ChatGPT models, such as in government, transportation, and hospitality.

Review of Practical Applications of ChatGPT Models in Industry Settings

ChatGPT models have been applied in various industries, and some of the most popular settings include customer service, content creation, and advertising.

In this in-depth review, we'll explore the practical applications of ChatGPT models in these settings, as well as some strategies for building and deploying ChatGPT models in an industry context.

Customer Service:

ChatGPT models have been widely used in customer service to improve response times and provide personalized support.

Banks, e-commerce platforms, and other customer-facing businesses have used ChatGPT models to assist customers in banking transactions, provide advice on financial products, and help customers with product information, order tracking, and returns. One of the advantages of ChatGPT models is their ability to provide real-time, conversational support to customers, which can improve customer satisfaction and reduce support costs for businesses.

To build and deploy ChatGPT models for customer service, businesses should focus on training their models on relevant customer data and optimizing the models for conversational accuracy and speed.

Additionally, businesses should consider integrating their ChatGPT models with other customer service technologies, such as voice assistants or chatbots, to provide a seamless and personalized support experience.

Content Creation:

ChatGPT models have been used to generate content across various industries, including journalism, marketing, and entertainment. News organizations have used ChatGPT models to automatically generate news articles on topics such as sports, finance, and weather.

Marketers have used ChatGPT models to generate social media posts and product descriptions. ChatGPT models have also been used to generate dialogue for video games and chatbots.

To build and deploy ChatGPT models for content creation, businesses should focus on training their models on relevant data sources and optimizing the models for accuracy and relevance to their target audience.

Additionally, businesses should consider integrating their ChatGPT models with other content creation technologies, such as image recognition or video editing software, to create a more holistic content generation process.

Advertising:

ChatGPT models have been used in advertising to personalize ads and improve targeting. ChatGPT models can analyze user data to create personalized ad campaigns that are more likely to resonate with individual users. Additionally, ChatGPT models can help businesses identify new target audiences based on user data and generate ad copy that is more likely to convert.

To build and deploy ChatGPT models for advertising, businesses should focus on training their models on relevant user data and optimizing the models for ad targeting and conversion. Additionally, businesses should consider integrating their ChatGPT models with other advertising technologies, such as ad networks or demand-side platforms, to create a more comprehensive advertising strategy.

ChatGPT models have demonstrated many potential applications in industry, and businesses can benefit from building and deploying ChatGPT models in various settings such as customer service, content creation, and advertising.

ChatGPT models have seen a wide range of practical applications in various industries. Here is a review of some of the practical applications of ChatGPT models in industry:

Content Generation:

ChatGPT models have been used to generate content across various industries, including journalism, marketing, and entertainment.

News organizations have used ChatGPT models to automatically generate news articles on topics such as sports, finance, and weather. Marketers have used ChatGPT models to generate social media posts and product descriptions. ChatGPT models have also been used to generate dialogue for video games and chatbots.

Healthcare:

ChatGPT models have been used to provide personalized healthcare support to patients.

For example, chatbots powered by ChatGPT models have been used to assist patients in scheduling appointments, provide medication reminders, and answer health-related questions. ChatGPT models have also been used to analyze medical records and suggest treatments for patients.

Finance:

ChatGPT models have been used in the finance industry to provide personalized financial advice and investment recommendations. Financial institutions have used ChatGPT models to provide investment advice, portfolio analysis, and budgeting assistance to their customers.

Education:

ChatGPT models have been used in education to provide personalized educational support to students. For example, chatbots powered by ChatGPT models have been used to provide explanations for complex concepts, assist students in completing assignments, and provide feedback on student work.

Legal Services:

ChatGPT models can be used to generate legal documents and contracts, reducing the time and cost associated with manual document creation. These models can also be used to provide legal advice and guidance to clients in real-time.

Human Resources:

ChatGPT models can be used to assist with recruitment by screening resumes, conducting initial interviews, and providing candidate feedback. These models can also be used to answer employee questions and provide training materials.

Financial Services:

ChatGPT models can be used to provide investment advice and portfolio management services, as well as answer customer questions about financial products and services.

Education:

ChatGPT models can be used to provide personalized learning experiences by generating quizzes, exercises, and assessments. These models can also be used to provide homework help and answer student questions.

Manufacturing:

ChatGPT models can be used to optimize production processes by analyzing sensor data and generating predictive maintenance schedules. These models can also be used to provide troubleshooting assistance to technicians.

Transportation:

ChatGPT models can be used to optimize logistics and supply chain management by analyzing data on shipping routes, inventory levels, and demand forecasts. These models can also be used to provide customer service and answer questions about shipping and delivery.

Hospitality:

ChatGPT models can be used to assist with hotel bookings, restaurant reservations, and event planning. These models can also be used to provide travel recommendations and answer customer questions about local attractions.

Energy:

ChatGPT models can be used to optimize energy production and distribution by analyzing data on weather patterns, energy demand, and production costs. These models can also be used to provide customer service and answer questions about energy usage and billing.

Public Safety:

ChatGPT models can be used to assist with emergency response by analyzing data on crime patterns, traffic flow, and weather conditions. These models can also be used to provide safety recommendations and answer citizen questions about public safety policies and procedures.

E-commerce:

ChatGPT models can be used to provide personalized product recommendations and shopping advice to customers, as well as answer questions about product availability, shipping, and returns.

Customer Service:

ChatGPT models can be used to automate customer service inquiries, providing quick and accurate responses to frequently asked questions. These models can also be used to escalate more complex inquiries to human agents.

Travel and Tourism:

ChatGPT models can be used to provide travel recommendations, help with itinerary planning, and answer questions about local attractions and customs. These models can also be used to assist with booking flights, hotels, and rental cars.

Media and Entertainment:

ChatGPT models can be used to create personalized content recommendations and assist with content creation, such as generating headlines or social media posts. These models can also be used to provide interactive experiences, such as chatbots for TV shows or movies.

Insurance:

ChatGPT models can be used to assist with claims processing, answering customer questions about policies and coverage, and providing personalized recommendations for insurance products.

Marketing and Advertising:

ChatGPT models can be used to optimize ad targeting and messaging, generate ad copy, and provide personalized recommendations for products or services. These models can also be used to engage with customers on social media and other channels.

Real Estate:

ChatGPT models can be used to assist with property searches, provide personalized recommendations for homes or apartments, and answer questions about real estate transactions.

Gaming:

ChatGPT models can be used to create personalized gaming experiences, such as generating custom quests or dialogue based on a player's behavior or preferences

These models can also be used to provide in-game support and troubleshooting assistance.

Agriculture:

ChatGPT models can be used to optimize crop yields and provide personalized recommendations for farming practices based on weather, soil conditions, and other factors.

These models can also be used to answer questions about agriculture regulations and best practices.

Sports:

ChatGPT models can be used to provide personalized recommendations for sports products or experiences, such as equipment or event tickets. These models can also be used to provide sports news updates and analysis, and answer fan questions about teams, players, and games.

Food and Beverage:

ChatGPT models can be used to provide personalized food and drink recommendations, such as recipe suggestions or restaurant recommendations. These models can also be used to assist with ordering and delivery inquiries.

Transportation:

ChatGPT models can be used to provide personalized transportation recommendations, such as route planning or ticket purchasing. These models can also be used to assist with customer inquiries about schedules, delays, and cancellations.

Energy and Utilities:

ChatGPT models can be used to provide personalized energy usage recommendations, such as tips for reducing energy consumption or optimizing energy efficiency. These models can also be used to assist with billing and payment inquiries.

Retail:

ChatGPT models can be used to provide personalized shopping recommendations, such as product suggestions or discounts. These models can also be used to assist with order tracking and customer support inquiries.

Nonprofits:

ChatGPT models can be used to assist with fundraising and donor engagement, providing personalized donation recommendations and answering questions about the organization's mission and impact.

These models can also be used to create interactive experiences, such as chatbots for volunteer recruitment.

Best Practices for Working with Stakeholders and End-Users

Best practices for working with stakeholders and end-users are critical for the successful deployment and adoption of ChatGPT models.

Here are some key practices to consider:

Involve Stakeholders And End-Users From The Beginning:
Engaging stakeholders and end-users from the beginning of the development process can ensure that their needs and concerns are taken into account.

This can be done through focus groups, surveys, or interviews to gather feedback and insights.

Establish Clear Goals And Objectives:
Clearly defining the goals and objectives of the ChatGPT model can help ensure that it is designed to meet the needs of stakeholders and end-users.

This can also help avoid scope creep or feature bloat that can lead to a less effective model.

Maintain Transparency And Communication:
Maintaining transparent communication throughout the development process can help build trust and foster collaboration among stakeholders and end-users.

This includes providing updates on progress and addressing concerns in a timely manner.

Incorporate Feedback And Iterate:
Incorporating feedback from stakeholders and end-users can help improve the quality and effectiveness of the ChatGPT model. Iterating on the model based on feedback can help ensure that it meets the needs of end-users and stakeholders.

Provide Appropriate Training And Support:
Providing appropriate training and support to end-users can help ensure that the ChatGPT model is used effectively and efficiently. This can include providing user guides, training sessions, and ongoing support.

Monitor Performance And Make Improvements:
 Monitoring the performance of the ChatGPT model and making improvements as needed can help ensure that it continues to meet the needs of end-users and stakeholders over time. This includes monitoring user feedback, usage statistics, and performance metrics.

By following these best practices, developers can ensure that ChatGPT models are designed and deployed in a way that meets the needs of stakeholders and end-users.

APPENDIX A:
GLOSSARY OF KEY TERMS

Attention-Based Summarization: A type of text summarization technique that uses an attention mechanism to identify the most important parts of a document to include in the summary.

Attention Mechanism: A mechanism in neural network architectures that allows the model to focus on specific parts of the input sequence. Attention mechanisms are commonly used in natural language processing tasks such as machine translation and summarization.

Backpropagation: A training algorithm used in neural networks that calculates the gradient of the loss function with respect to the model's parameters. Backpropagation is used to update the model's parameters during training.

Bidirectional Encoder Representations from Transformers (BERT): A pre-trained language model developed by Google that uses a transformer-based architecture similar to ChatGPT. BERT is commonly used for tasks such as question answering and sentiment analysis.

Conditional Generation: A type of text generation where the generated text is conditioned on some input, such as a prompt or a sequence of words. ChatGPT is an example of a model capable of conditional generation.

Contextual Embedding: A representation of a word or phrase in a way that takes into account the context in which it appears, often using neural network models such as transformers.

Dependency Parsing: A natural language processing task that involves identifying the grammatical relationships between words in a sentence.

Dialogue Act:A unit of conversation that describes the intended purpose of a speaker's utterance, such as a request for information or an apology. Dialogue act recognition is a task in natural language processing used to identify these units.

Distributional Semantics:A framework for representing the meaning of words based on their distribution in a corpus of text.

Embedding:A technique used in natural language processing to represent words or tokens as vectors of numerical values. Embeddings capture semantic relationships between words, such as similarity or relatedness.

Encoder-Decoder Architecture:A type of neural network architecture commonly used in natural language processing tasks such as machine translation and text summarization.

Entity Linking:A natural language processing task that involves identifying named entities in text and linking them to their corresponding entries in a knowledge base. Entity linking is commonly used in applications such as question answering and information extraction.

Fine-Tuning: The process of retraining a pre-trained model on a specific task or domain. Fine-tuning is a common technique used to adapt pre-trained language models, such as ChatGPT, to specific use cases.

Generative Model:A type of machine learning model that is used to generate new data, such as text or images. Generative models, such as ChatGPT, learn to generate data by modeling the probability distribution of the data.

Hyperparameter:A parameter that is set before training a machine learning model and controls the behavior of the model. Examples of hyperparameters include learning rate, batch size, and number of layers in a neural network.

Inference: The process of using a trained model to generate predictions or generate new data, such as text. Inference involves feeding input data into the model and using its learned parameters to generate output.

Language Modeling:A natural language processing task that involves predicting the probability distribution of the next word in a sequence given the previous words. Language modeling is used to train language models, including ChatGPT.

Multi-Head Attention:A mechanism used in the Transformer architecture, which allows the model to attend to different parts of the input sequence at the same time. This helps the model capture more complex relationships between words in the input sequence.

Named Entity Recognition (NER):A natural language processing task that involves identifying and classifying named entities in text, such as names of people, organizations, and locations. NER is commonly used in applications such as information extraction and question answering.

Natural Language Generation (NLG):A subfield of natural language processing that focuses on generating human-like language from computer systems. NLG can be used to generate text for various applications, including chatbots and content creation.

Natural Language Understanding (NLU):A subfield of natural language processing that focuses on the analysis of natural language input to extract meaning and enable the processing of text by computers.

Perplexity:A measure of how well a language model predicts a given sequence of words, based on the degree of uncertainty in the model's predictions.

Preprocessing: The process of preparing raw text data for use in natural language processing tasks. Preprocessing may involve tasks such as tokenization, cleaning, and normalization.

Recurrent Neural Network (RNN):A type of neural network architecture commonly used in natural language processing tasks. RNNs are designed to process sequential data and can capture long-term dependencies between words in a sequence.

Recurrent Neural Network Language Model (RNNLM):
A type of language model that uses recurrent neural network architecture to model the probability distribution of the next word in a sequence, based on the previous words.

Reinforcement Learning: A type of machine learning where an agent learns to take actions in an environment in order to maximize a reward signal. Reinforcement learning is used in natural language processing applications such as dialog systems and chatbots.

Seq2Seq: A type of neural network architecture used in natural language processing tasks such as machine translation and summarization. Seq2Seq models are designed to process input sequences and generate output sequences.

Sequence Labeling: A natural language processing task that involves assigning labels to each element in a sequence, such as part-of-speech tagging or named entity recognition.

Sequence-to-Sequence (Seq2Seq) Model: A neural network architecture that is commonly used for natural language processing tasks such as machine translation and text summarization. Seq2Seq models consist of an encoder and a decoder, which work together to generate a target sequence from a source sequence.

Sentiment Analysis: A natural language processing task that involves analyzing text to determine the sentiment or emotional tone of the text. Sentiment analysis is commonly used in applications such as social media monitoring and customer feedback analysis.

Text Classification: A natural language processing task that involves categorizing text into predefined categories, such as spam/not spam or positive/negative sentiment. Text classification is used in various applications, including sentiment analysis and topic modeling.

Tokenization: The process of breaking up text into individual units, or tokens, such as words or subwords. Tokenization is a common preprocessing step in natural language processing tasks.

Topic Modeling:A natural language processing task that involves identifying the underlying topics in a collection of text documents. Topic modeling is commonly used in applications such as text classification and content recommendation.

Transformer:A neural network architecture used in natural language processing tasks such as language modeling, machine translation, and question answering. The Transformer architecture uses multi-head attention and positional encoding to capture complex relationships between words in a sequence.

Universal Sentence Encoder (USE):A pre-trained sentence encoder developed by Google that can be used for a variety of natural language processing tasks, such as text classification and sentiment analysis. USE is based on a transformer-based architecture similar to ChatGPT.

Unsupervised Learning:A type of machine learning where a model is trained on unlabeled data, without any explicit supervision or labels. Unsupervised learning is used in natural language processing tasks such as clustering and word embeddings.

Word Embedding:A technique used in natural language processing to represent words or tokens as vectors of numerical values. Word embeddings capture the semantic meaning of words and are used as input to many natural language processing models.

Word Sense Disambiguation:A natural language processing task that involves identifying the correct meaning of a word in context, when the word has multiple possible meanings.

APPENDIX B
REFERENCES

Vaswani, A., Shazeer, N., Parmar, N., Uszkoreit, J., Jones, L., Gomez, A. N., ... & Polosukhin, I. (2017). Attention is all you need. In Advances in neural information processing systems (pp. 5998-6008).

Brown, T. B., Mann, B., Ryder, N., Subbiah, M., Kaplan, J., Dhariwal, P., ... & Amodei, D. (2020). Language models are few-shot learners. In Advances in Neural Information Processing Systems (pp. 1877-1901).

Radford, A., Wu, J., Child, R., Luan, D., Amodei, D., & Sutskever, I. (2019). Language models are unsupervised multitask learners. OpenAI Blog, 1(8), 9.

Mikolov, T., Chen, K., Corrado, G., & Dean, J. (2013). Efficient estimation of word representations in vector space. arXiv preprint arXiv:1301.3781.

Pennington, J., Socher, R., & Manning, C. D. (2014). Glove: Global vectors for word representation. In Proceedings of the 2014 conference on empirical methods in natural language processing (EMNLP) (pp. 1532-1543).

Hochreiter, S., & Schmidhuber, J. (1997). Long short-term memory. Neural computation, 9(8), 1735-1780.

Cho, K., Van Merriënboer, B., Gulcehre, C., Bahdanau, D., Bougares, F., Schwenk, H., & Bengio, Y. (2014). Learning phrase representations using RNN encoder-decoder for statistical machine translation. arXiv preprint arXiv:1406.1078.

Kim, Y. (2014). Convolutional neural networks for sentence classification. arXiv preprint arXiv:1408.5882.

Johnson, R., & Zhang, T. (2015). Semi-supervised convolutional neural networks for text categorization via region embedding. In Advances in neural information processing systems (pp. 919-927).

Collobert, R., Weston, J., Bottou, L., Karlen, M., Kavukcuoglu, K., & Kuksa, P. (2011). Natural language processing (almost) from scratch. Journal of Machine Learning Research, 12(Aug), 2493-2537.

Devlin, J., Chang, M. W., Lee, K., & Toutanova, K. (2018). Bert: Pre-training of deep bidirectional transformers for language understanding. arXiv preprint arXiv:1810.04805.

www.ingramcontent.com/pod-product-compliance
Lightning Source LLC
Chambersburg PA
CBHW080837310526
45796CB00015B/301